ACCESS
SPANISH

María Utrera Cejudo

Series editor: **Jane Wightwick**

Hodder Arnold
A MEMBER OF THE HODDER HEADLINE GROUP

Orders: please contact Bookpoint Ltd, 130 Milton Park, Abingdon, Oxon OX14 4SB.
Telephone: (44) 01235 827720. Fax: (44) 01235 400454. Lines are open from 9.00 to 6.00,
Monday to Saturday, with a 24-hour message answering service. You can also order through our
website www.hoddereducation.co.uk.

British Library Cataloguing in Publication Data
A catalogue record for this title is available from the British Library

ISBN-10 0 34081675 9
ISBN-13 978 0 34081675 2

First Published 2004
Impression number   10 9 8 7 6 5 4
Year   2010 2009 2008 2007 2006

Typeset by Hardlines Ltd, Charlbury, Oxford.
Illustrations by Jon Davis/Linden Artists, Marco Schaaf/NB Illustration, Illustrated Arts
Printed in Dubai for Hodder Arnold, an imprint of Hodder Education, a division of Hodder Headline,
338 Euston Road, London NW1 3BH.

ACKNOWLEDGEMENTS

The authors and publishers would like to thank the following for use of their material in this volume:

AC Hotels for hotel details (Costa Meloneras & Gran Canaria) on pages 126-7; anthonys.com/Oscar de la Renta for web page p.64; Argentina turismo for web page p.178; Callejero Lanetra for maps of Madrid and surroundings (pages 88, 90, 95, 96); Caribe Mexicano for web page p.136; Adolfo Dominguez for web page p.63; www.elmundomaya.com for web page p.138; geocities.com/Venezuela for web page p.45; guiadelmondo.com for web page p.27; Panorama: Reportajes for article from www.laverdad.es page 148; www.turismo.sevilla.org for map of Seville centre page 105; www.visitcostarica.com for web page p.159; Yahoo España on page 1.

Every effort has been made to trace and acknowledge ownership of copyright. The publishers will be glad to make suitable arrangements with any copyright holders whom it has not been possible to contact.

Photo acknowledgements

Alamy p.70 top, p.80, p.81, p.98 top right. C. Baldwin p.7 a & b, p.8, p.14. Corbis: p.16 a (Walter Hodges), p.16 b (Tom & Dee Ann McCarthy), p.17 c (Catherine Kurnow), p.17 d (Rob Lewine), p.17 e (Annebieque Bernard), p17 f (LWA-JDC), p.17 h (Paul Edmonson), p.44 (Stephen Welstead), p.65 (Lawrence Manning), p.77 (Michael Boys), p.98 centre right (Philippe Petit-Mars), p.98 bottom right, p.108 (Nik Wheeler), p.147 B (Jim Cummins), p.169 (PBNJ), p.175 (Bettmann), p.176 Frida Kahlo and Allende (Bettmann). Dorling Kindersley p.76 2nd from left. Empics p.21 (Pelé & Maradona), p.179 left. Getty Images p.98 bottom left. Life File/Emma Lee p.51, p.59, p.70 2nd from top, p.74 (Xavier Catalan), p.77. J. Lowe p.166 (bottom). Rex Features: p.17 g (R. Williamson), p.20 (Steve Wood/Sipa Press/Charles Sykes), p.21 Gwyneth Paltrow (Matt Barron), p.21 Gloria Estefan (Ken McKay), p.42 1, 2 & 5 (Mirek Towski), 3 (Vinnie Zuffante), 4 (Charles Sykes), 6 (C.Contino), p.45 (Sipa Press), p.49 bottom (Polydoros Anastesselis), p.54, p.70 2nd from bottom (Sipa Press), p.76 soup, p.165 (Sipa Press), p.176 top (Action Press), p.179 right (Sipa Press). M. Strang p.132, p.142, p.149, p.154, p.177 left. Rebecca Teevan p.94, p.118 (top), p.119, p.157. A. Woodman p.7 c, p.24, p.37.

All other photographs provided by the author and editors.

Cover photos: Corbis. Main image © Stephanie Colasanti, top right © Jose Fuste Raga, bottom left © Abilio Lope.

INTRODUCTION

Access Spanish is a refreshing, modern introduction to the Spanish language, culture and people. It is specially designed for adults of all ages who are just starting out learning Spanish or who are returning after a long gap.

The course is ideal for use in classes, but will also help develop strategies for independent learning. In the coursebook, teachers and learners will find an extended range of activities covering all four skills, as well as ideas for group activities.

A further range of ideas, activities, tips and advice is available on our website, www.accesslanguages.com. You don't have to use the site to benefit from the course but, according to your particular needs or interests, you will find a great deal of extra practice, information and links to useful Spanish sites. For more depth in a particular language structure, for example, we have included additional printable worksheets and we've even included advice and links for the major examinations and qualifications.

Access Spanish offers a fun and friendly approach to the Spanish language as it is spoken throughout the world today. It will enable you to deal with everyday situations, covering practical topics such as travel, shopping, making a complaint at a hotel or eating in a restaurant, and many of the activities are based on genuine Spanish websites. The course is also ideal for those who wish to study Spanish for business purposes and will provide learners with a sound basis of vocabulary and grammar structures.

The coursebook is divided into ten carefully graded units. At the beginning of each, the content and objectives are clearly identified and you can check your progress at various points throughout the unit. Each unit starts with a number of activities relating to the previous one so you can revise topics already covered, giving you the confidence to move on to new areas.

The units offer a wide range of activities which will quickly enable you to start reading and writing contemporary Spanish, and the listening exercises featuring authentic Spanish-speakers are integral to the course.

Each unit consists of:

- a checklist of topics covered in the unit

- revision activities (*¿Qué recuerdas?*): these give you the chance to revise important points covered in the previous unit

- listening activities: authentic conversations, passages and exercises to increase your listening skills and to help you acquire confidence

- speaking activities

- reading activities: authentic documents and exercises to extend your vocabulary and comprehension

- writing activities: practical and authentic forms to complete, grammar activities and letter-writing to consolidate key points and to reinforce confidence when travelling to a Spanish-speaking country

- exercises and games to work on with a partner

- exercises and games to work on with a group in order to practise the language through various practical situations

- games to be played with a partner or in a group

- **LANGUAGE FOCUS** Language Focus panels: these offer brief and concise structural and grammatical summaries with related activities

- **LEARNING TIP:** containing useful linguistic and cultural information

- frequent reviews, enabling you to check your progress and to feel confident in what you have learnt

- sections throughout the units covering individual linguistic differences in Latin American countries

-  special sections at the end of each unit giving general information and related activities on Spanish-speaking countries around the world

- **GLOSSARY** Spanish-English glossaries containing vocabulary used in the unit

- **LOOKING FORWARD** preparation and dictionary skills ready for the next unit

- links to our dedicated website www.accesslanguages.com containing extra activities to practise key points, useful links to Spanish sites and advice on further study and examinations

Answers to the exercises and full recording transcripts are available in a separate Support Booklet, and we strongly recommend that you obtain the **Access Spanish Support Book and Audio Pack** (CD or cassette version), which will enable you to develop your listening skills and get used to hearing the Spanish language as it is spoken now.

We hope that working through this course will be an enjoyable experience and that you will find this new approach to language learning fun.

ACCESS SPANISH

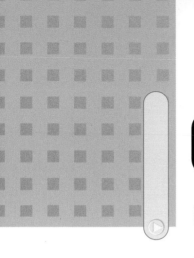

CONTENTS

UNIT 1
¡Hola!

By the end of this unit you will be able to:

- Say hello and goodbye
- Introduce yourself
- Understand different ways of greeting and react accordingly
- Ask and understand simple questions
- Say where you live and where you are from
- Say and recognise the Spanish alphabet
- Count from 1 to 15

Recognising words or phrases in Spanish is not always as difficult as it seems. The Internet age has hugely accelerated the integration of English into the Spanish language. You only need a few words to start with to find your way around. Prove this to yourself by listening to a Spanish dialogue straight away.

1 ¿Empezamos? (Shall we start?)

A Listen to the dialogue and tick the information asked for. Don't worry about understanding every word – just see if you can get the gist.

◯	**Name**	◯	**Profession**
◯	**Nationality**	◯	**Marital status**
◯	**Address**	◯	**Telephone no.**

B Listen to the dialogue again and put the following words in the right order:

1 ¿nombre es cuál su?

2 ¿su cuál es dirección?

3 ¿es profesión cuál su?

4 ¿nacionalidad es cuál su?

Did you pick out the answers to the questions in the dialogue?

C Now work in pairs and ask your partner what his or her name is. When you are asked, the reply is: **Me llamo** ...

Note the other way of asking for someone's name:

¿Cómo se llama?

In the following units, we will see other ways of asking for personal information such as:

¿De dónde es? (*Where are you from?*)

¿Qué hace? (*What do you do?*)

If you did not catch an answer and you want the person to repeat it, say:

¿Perdón? or **¿Puede repetir, por favor?**

D Listen to the dialogue and fill in the gaps using the words below:

Yo   nombre   apellido   llamo   Encantado

A Buenas tardes, me ⟨＿＿＿⟩ Carmen González. Mi ⟨＿＿＿⟩ es Carmen y mi ⟨＿＿＿⟩ es González.

B ⟨＿＿＿⟩ me llamo Paco López.

A Encantada.

B ⟨＿＿＿⟩.

LANGUAGE FOCUS

In Spanish, you have to change the end of the verb, depending on who you are speaking about:

(Yo) me llam**o** …	*My name is …*
(Tú) te llam**as** …	*Your name is …*
(Usted) se llam**a** …	*Your name is …*
(Él) se llam**a** …	*His name is …*
(Ella) se llam**a** …	*Her name is …*

Notice that if you try to translate word for word, the expressions don't always make sense.

Me llamo Carmen. = My name is Carmen.
(literally: 'myself call Carmen')

2 ¿*Usted* o *tú*? (*Usted* or *Tú*?)

A Mix and Match game. Your teacher will give you a card with a name on it. Go around the class and find your other half (for example, Adam–Eve). Look at the words to help you. Listen to the example:

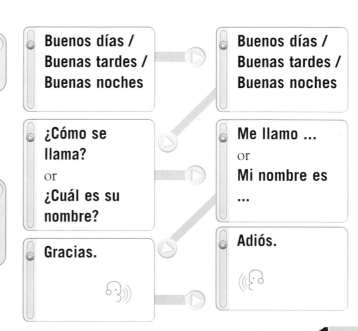

Buenos días / Buenas tardes / Buenas noches	Buenos días / Buenas tardes / Buenas noches
¿Cómo se llama? or ¿Cuál es su nombre?	Me llamo … or Mi nombre es …
Gracias.	Adiós.

LEARNING TIP:
How are you?

When greeting a relative, friend or someone you know well, address them informally:

Hola, ¿qué tal? / ¿cómo estás?
Hello, how are you?

But if it is someone you know less well or not at all, say:

Buenos días / Buenas tardes / Buenas noches, ¿cómo está?
Good morning/afternoon/evening, how are you?

The reply will be: **Muy bien, ¿y tú? / ¿y usted?**

Muy bien (☺☺☺) means *Very well*. Other possible replies are:

Bien (☺☺)	*Well*
Regular (☺)	*So-so*
Mal (☹)	*Not too good*
Fatal (☹☹)	*Terrible*

Try the additional activity on www.accesslanguages.com

B When you have done this, repeat the same activity using the informal form.

¿Cómo te llamas? or **¿Cuál es tu nombre?**

C What would you say in these situations?

1 You bump into an old friend one night in a disco.

2 You are out shopping one morning and you meet a work colleague.

3 You are in the park one afternoon and you meet your young niece.

4 You bump into your boss one evening in a bar.

5 You greet an elderly neighbour one morning on your way to work.

D How will the people answer? Write what you think they will say (use the symbols to help you).

1 ☺☺☺ **2** ☺ **3** ☹☹ **4** ☺☺ **5** ☹

E 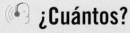 Listen to the situations and for each one, mark whether it is formal or informal and whether it takes place in the morning or afternoon/evening.

	formal	informal	a.m	p.m.
1				
2				
3				
4				
5				

3 Los números (Numbers)

A 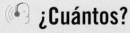 Listen to the lottery numbers and tick the ones you hear.

Sorteo	Número ganador		Sorteo	Número ganador	
ONCE	78426	☐	ONCE	93578	☐
ONCE	57692	☐	ONCE	68462	☐
ONCE	63714	☐	ONCE	73914	☐

• • • • O N C E • • •

LANGUAGE FOCUS

¿Cuántos?

uno	dos	tres	cuatro	cinco	seis	siete	ocho	nueve	diez

B ✏ ▶ Complete the form below with your own details.

Hotel Montecristo

Apellidos	⬭	Nombre	⬭
Dirección	⬭	Provincia	⬭
	⬭	Código Postal	⬭
Teléfono	⬭	Teléfono móvil	⬭

LANGUAGE FOCUS

To ask for somebody's name, you can say:

¿Cuál	es	su	nombre?
What	is	your	name?

You can ask many more questions using the same model:
- What is your address?
- What is your telephone number? etc.

C 🗣 🧠 ▶ Work with a partner. Ask him or her for the information needed to complete the form in activity 3B.

¿Cúal es su/tu … ?

When you have finished, swap roles.

LANGUAGE FOCUS

🎧 **Más números**

13 trece

12 DOCE

11 once

14 catorce

15 quince

D 🎧 Write any five numbers from one to fifteen in the boxes below. Listen and tick the ones you hear. The first person to tick all five numbers says 'Bingo!'.

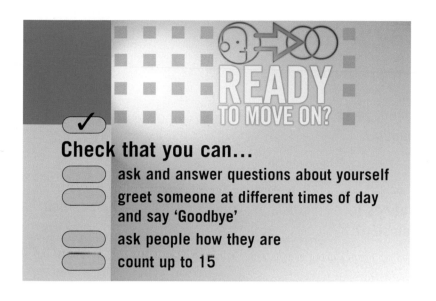

Check that you can...

ask and answer questions about yourself

greet someone at different times of day
and say 'Goodbye'

ask people how they are

count up to 15

4 ¿Quién soy? (Who am I?)

A Look at the four people below and listen to them introduce themselves in Spanish. Can you work out who's who?

Holgar   Carmen
Marie   Fabio

a

Spanish mechanic from Madrid

b

German from Berlin lives in Edinburgh

c

French student born in Paris

d

Italian architect lives in Rome

B Now look at the sentences below; can you guess what each one means?

1 Soy mecánica.   3 Soy de Berlín.   5 Soy francesa.

2 Soy española.   4 Vivo en Edimburgo.   6 Soy arquitecto.

C Match the sentences in activity 4B to the people in activity 4A.

¡Hola! UNIT 1

ACCESS SPANISH

You can find more practice of these verb at www.accesslanguages.co

5 Preguntas (Questions)

A Look and listen.

Carmen, ¿eres española?

Sí, soy española, de Madrid.

¿Cuál es tu profesión?

Soy mecánica.

¿Vives en Madrid?

Sí, vivo en Madrid.

Holgar, ¿es español?

No, soy alemán, de Berlín.

¿Vive en Berlín?

No, vivo en Edimburgo.

Spanish mechanic from Madrid

German from Berlin lives in Edinburgh

B Now practise with Marie and Fabio by asking the same questions.

LANGUAGE FOCUS

ser – *to be*

(yo) **soy**	*I am*
(tú) **eres**	*you are* (informal)
(usted) **es**	*you are* (formal)
(él) **es**	*he is*
(ella) **es**	*she is*

vivir – *to live*

(yo) viv**o**	*I live*
(tú) viv**es**	*you live* (informal)
(usted) viv**e**	*you live* (formal)
(él) viv**e**	*he lives*
(ella) viv**e**	*she lives*

Ejemplos:

(Yo) **soy** Karen.
(Yo) viv**o** en Londres.
Soy inglesa.
Soy de Londres.
Soy mecánica.

Ken **es** estadounidense.
Ken viv**e** en Nueva York.
Es de Chicago.
Y tú, ¿de dónde **eres**?   ¿Dónde viv**es**?
Y usted, ¿de dónde **es**?   ¿Dónde viv**e**?

C Work with a partner and find out the following information by asking him/her questions in Spanish. Then swap roles.

Name	
Nationality	
Profession	
Address	
Telephone	

D Listen to three people being interviewed and complete the table.

Nombre	Pablo	Dieter	Jean
Nacionalidad	SPANISH	GERMAN	FRENCH
Profesión	STUDENT	STUDENT	ARCHITECT
Teléfono	982226397		0142753528

E Compare your answers with those of your partner. Did you get all the information?

¡Hola! UNIT 1

LEARNING TIP:
The 'letters' *ch*, *ll* and *rr*

The letter combinations **ch**, **ll** and **rr** used to be considered as separate letters in the Spanish alphabet, with their own sections in the dictionary. Now, however, they are incorporated into **c**, **l** and **r**, as in English, but they still have their own sounds: **che**, **elle** and **erre**.

Accents in Spanish

The acute accent (´) is used in Spanish to show where a word is stressed. When spelling words out, you say **con acento** after the letter carrying the accent:

alemán = a-l-e-m-a con acento n

For more activities on this unit, go to our website www.accesslanguages.com

Check that you can...
- say who you are
- say your nationality, the place you come from and where you live
- say what you do

6 El abecedario (The alphabet)

A Listen to and repeat the alphabet.

a b c ch d e f g h i j k l ll m n ñ o p q r rr s t u v w x y z

B ¿Cómo se escribe? Listen how different people are asked to spell their surnames. Tick the ones you hear in the box:

- ( ) Hernández
- (2) Martínez
- (3) García
- (1) Fernández
- ( ) Martín
- ( ) Gracia

C Work with a partner. Your teacher will give you a card with a set of words like the ones below. Spell your words to your partner, then write your partner's words in the space provided on the card.

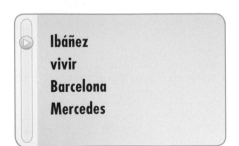

Ibáñez
vivir
Barcelona
Mercedes

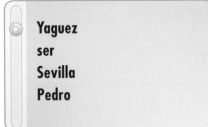

Yaguez
ser
Sevilla
Pedro

Descubre el mundo HISPANO

At the end of each unit, we will go around the world and discover different Spanish-speaking countries.

A [A¢] ▷ Look at the map and the article below. Can you list all the Spanish-speaking countries?

B [A¢] ▷ Where is Spanish spoken in the United States?

Colombia *new mexico*
colorado *Arizona* *Texas*

C [A¢] ▷ In which countries is Spanish not the main language?

Brazil	⬭ ✓	Canada	⬭ ✓
Bahamas	⬭ ✓	Haiti	⬭ ✓
Dominican Republic	⬭	Argentina	⬭

(🔊) La lengua española no sólo se habla en España, sino también en Andorra, Argentina, Bolivia, Chile, Colombia, Costa Rica, Cuba, Ecuador, El Salvador, España, Estados Unidos, Filipinas, Guatemala, Guinea Ecuatorial, Haití, Honduras, Jamaica, México, Nicaragua, Panamá, Paraguay, Perú, Puerto Rico, República Dominicana, Sáhara, Uruguay, Venezuela. En los Estados Unidos se habla en diferentes territorios de California, Nuevo México, Colorado, Arizona, Tejas. También hay personas que utilizan la lengua española en Nueva York, y en el estado de Florida.

Relación de Países Hispanohablantes

Océano Pacífico · América del norte · Océano Atlántico · Europa · Asia · Océano Pacífico · África · Océano Índico · Oceanía · América del sur

UNIT **1**

11

GLOSSARY

Nouns

apellido (m)	surname
arquitecto/a (m/f)	architect
código postal (m)	postcode
dirección (f)	address
Edimburgo	Edinburgh
estudiante (m/f)	student
lengua (f)	language
Londres	London
mecánico/a (m/f)	mechanic
nacionalidad (f)	nationality
nombre (m)	(first) name
París	Paris
profesión (f)	profession
profesor(a) (m/f)	teacher
provincia (f)	province, county
Roma	Rome
señor (m)	sir, Mr
señora (f)	madam, Mrs
señorita (f)	miss, Miss
teléfono (m)	telephone (number)

Adjectives

alemán/alemana	German
bien	well
español(a)	Spanish
estadounidense	American/from the USA
fatal	terrible
francés/francesa	French
inglés/inglesa	English
italiano/a	Italian

mal	not too good
muy bien	very well
regular	so-so
su	your (formal)
tu	your (informal)

Verbs

llamarse	to be called
ser	to be
vivir	to live

Pronouns

él	he
ella	she
tú	you (informal)
usted	you (formal)
yo	I

Expressions

Adiós.	Goodbye.
Buenas noches.	Good night.
Buenas tardes.	Good afternoon.
Buenos días.	Good morning./Hello.
¿Cómo está?	How are you? (formal)
¿Cómo estás?	How are you? (informal)
¿Cómo se escribe ... ?	How do you spell ...?
¿Cómo se llama?	What's your name? (formal)
¿Cuál es ...?	What is ...?

GLOSSARY

¿De dónde eres?	Where are you from? (informal)
¿De dónde es?	Where are you from? (formal)
Encantado/a.	Pleased to meet you.
Gracias.	Thank you.
¡Hola!	Hello!
¿Perdón?	Pardon?
¿Puede repetir, por favor?	Can you repeat, please?
¿Qué tal?	How are you? (informal)
sí/no	yes/no

Prepositions

de	from, of
en	in, on

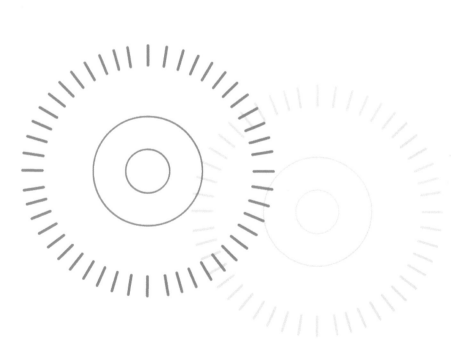

LOOKING FORWARD

In **Unit 2**, we will be looking at more nationalities, occupations and languages.

To prepare, look at the list of nationalities and jobs below and see if you can work out what they mean.

Nacionalidades

- británico • canadiense • escocés
- americano • galés • australiano
- irlandés • estadounidense

Profesiones

- estudiante • oficinista • profesor
- abogado • secretaria • ingeniero
- director • contable • médico

UNIT 2
Otra gente y yo

¡Hola!

UNIT 2
Otra gente y yo

By the end of this unit you will be able to:

- Say more about nationalities
- Say what language you speak
- Say what you do for a living and where you work
- Count up to 99
- Ask for a phone number and give yours
- Say your age
- Find out more details about someone

1 ¿Qué recuerdas?

A Match the following expressions:

1	What is your name?	**a**	Soy estudiante.
2	Good afternoon.	**b**	¿Cuál es tu nacionalidad?
3	I am a student.	**c**	Buenas tardes.
4	I live in Paris.	**d**	¿Cómo te llamas?
5	Where are you from?	**e**	Vivo en París.
6	Could you repeat that, please?	**f**	¿Puede repetir, por favor?
7	How are you?	**g**	¿Cómo se escribe?
8	How do you spell that?	**h**	¿Cómo estás?

2

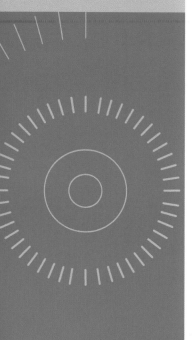

B 🔊)) 🎧 ▷ Lynn is an American student from Santa Mónica in California who lives and studies Spanish in Mexico City.

1 What questions would you ask Lynn to find out this information?

2 How would she answer these questions?

3 Imagine you are Lynn. How would you introduce yourself?

4 Now listen and check.

C ✏️ ▷ Write a question for each of these answers.

1 Se llama Joaquín.

2 Vive en Barcelona.

3 Es español, de Gerona.

4 Es arquitecto.

5 Me llamo Ana.

6 Soy de Londres.

2 ¿Qué haces / hace?

A 🎲 ▷ Match the jobs with the pictures.

1 profesor(a)

a

2 secretario/a

b

c

3 médico

4 enfermero/a

d

e

5 oficinista

6 abogado/a

f

g

7 recepcionista

8 camarero/a

h

LEARNING TIP:
Asking about occupations

In Unit 1, you saw how to ask someone's occupation using the expression **¿Cuál es tu/su profesión?**

Another very common way to ask the same question is by saying:

¿Qué haces? (informal)

¿Qué hace? (formal)

Gender

In Unit 1, you saw that most words for jobs change according to the gender of the person concerned. Objects are also masculine or feminine:

la mesa *the table*

el libro *the book*

In general, if a noun ends in **o**, it is masculine, and if it ends in **a**, it is feminine. You'll find more about noun endings in Unit 4.

Note that some nouns do not change:

recepcionista *receptionist* (male or female)

médico *doctor* (male or female)

Articles

In Spanish, the words for *a* or *an* are not used when talking about jobs or occupations.

Soy profesor. (not Soy un profesor.)

B Now look at the pictures and answer the question **¿Qué hace(s)?** for each picture. Remember to use the correct gender for the picture.

Example: **a** ¿Qué haces? —Soy enfermer**a**.

Otra gente y yo

2

LANGUAGE FOCUS

The verb **trabajar** is a regular verb. Other verbs that end in **–ar** follow a similar pattern.

Notice that the endings for **–ar** verbs are slightly different from those for **–ir** verbs (see the verb **vivir** in Unit 1).

trabajar *to work*

(yo)	trabaj**o**	*I work*
(tú)	trabaj**as**	*you work* (informal)
(usted)	trabaj**a**	*you work* (formal)
(él)	trabaj**a**	*he works*
(ella)	trabaj**a**	*she works*

C Say where each of the people in activity 2A works. Use the words in the box:

| colegio | oficina | clínica | hospital | bar | tribunal | hotel |

Example: **a** Soy profesor, **trabajo en** un colegio.

D Fill in the gaps in this conversation with the appropriate form of **trabajar** (remember always to look for the person the verb refers to). Then listen and check your answers.

Carmen: Julia, ¿ (　　　　) en una oficina?

Julia: No, (　　　　) en un banco.

Carmen: Y Carlos, ¿ (　　　　) contigo?

Julia: No, no (　　　　) conmigo. Y tú, ¿ (　　　　) en un hospital?

Carmen: Sí, (　　　　) en el hospital de "La Paz".

3 ¿De dónde eres / es?

LANGUAGE FOCUS

 1  2  3

Spanish adjectives agree in gender and number with the nouns they go with. The form you see in the dictionary is usually the masculine singular. To make the feminine form, you need to note the following:

1 Adjectives ending in –o change to –a
chin**o** → chin**a**

2 Those ending in –e or –u do not change
estadounidens**e** → estadounidens**e**

3 Most adjectives ending in a consonant add –**a**
español → español**a**

Adjectives (including nationalities) that have an accent on the last syllable lose the accent in the feminine form:
japon**és** → japon**esa**   ingl**és** → ingl**esa**

A ⒶⒸ ▶ Many names of countries are similar in English and Spanish. Can you match the English with the Spanish?

1	Canada	**a**	Italia	6	Philippines	**f**	Canadá
2	Cuba	**b**	Japón	7	Japan	**g**	Bolivia
3	Bolivia	**c**	Rusia	8	Russia	**h**	Francia
4	Argentina	**d**	Argentina	9	France	**i**	Brasil
5	Brazil	**e**	Cuba	10	Italy	**j**	Filipinas

¿Cuál es tu nacionalidad? ¿Eres español? Another very common way to ask the same question is by saying:

¿De dónde eres? (in informal situations, i.e. when you are with family, friends, or younger people)

¿De dónde es? (in formal situations, i.e. when you are with people older than you or someone you do not know very well)

Remember that in Spanish, when talking about nationalities, most of the endings change depending on the gender of the person or thing being described.

Note that, in Spanish, you don't need to use capital letters for nationalities.

B ✍ ▷ Now match the countries in activity 3A with the nationalities, then make them feminine.

1 brasileño   **2** japonés   **3** canadiense   **4** argentino   **5** cubano
6 filipino   **7** italiano   **8** francés   **9** ruso   **10** boliviano

C 🎧 ▷ Listen to three people talking about themselves, then look at the sentences below. Some details are wrong. Can you say which are right and which are wrong, then correct the mistakes?

1 Carmen es secretaria, trabaja en una oficina. Es española, de Barcelona, pero vive en Madrid.

2 Juan es camarero, trabaja en un restaurante. Es chileno, de Santiago, y vive en Santiago.

3 Lynn es estudiante, estudia español en la universidad de México. Es estadounidense, de California, pero vive en Ciudad de México.

LEARNING TIP:

The masculine form of the nationality is used for the corresponding language:

inglés   English
francés   French
español   Spanish

4 ¿Qué lenguas hablas / habla?

A 🎲 ▷ Match pictures of these famous people with their nationalities and native language. (Remember to make the nationality adjective agree!)

Claudia Schiffer

Robbie Williams

Antonio Banderas

LANGUAGE FOCUS

The verb **hablar** uses the same endings as **trabajar**.

(yo)	habl**o**	*I speak*
(tú)	habl**as**	*you speak* (informal)
(usted)	habl**a**	*you speak* (formal)
(él)	habl**a**	*he speaks*
(ella)	habl**a**	*she speaks*

Gwyneth Paltrow

Pelé

Maradona

Nationalities

| español(a)   alemán (–ana)   estadounidense   argentino/a   inglés (–esa)   brasileño/a |

Languages

| español   inglés   alemán   portugués |

Person	Nationality	Language
Claudia Schiffer		

B  Now write a small paragraph about the famous people in activity 4A.

Me llamo Gloria. Soy cubana, pero vivo en Florida. Soy cantante y hablo español, inglés y un poco de portugués.

READY TO MOVE ON?

✓

Check that you can...

- ask and answer about what you and others do for a living
- ask and answer about where you and others work
- ask and answer about nationality
- ask and answer about what languages you and others speak

LEARNING TIP:
pero = but

2

5 Más números

LANGUAGE FOCUS

16	17	18	19
dieciséis	diecisiete	dieciocho	diecinueve
20	21	22	23
veinte	veintiuno	veintidós	veintitrés
30	31	32	33
treinta	treinta y uno	treinta y dos	treinta y tres
40	41	42	43
cuarenta	cuarenta y uno	cuarenta y dos	cuarenta y tres
50	51	52	53
cincuenta	cincuenta y uno	cincuenta y dos	cincuenta y tres
60	70	80	90
sesenta	setenta	ochenta	noventa

The numbers from 0 to 30 are written as one word, e.g. **veintitrés**.
From 31, the numbers are written separately with **y** (*and*), e.g. **setenta y seis**.

When the phone rings in Spain, you answer by saying **¿Dígame?**

In Peru and Chile, you say **¿Aló?**

In Colombia, it's **A ver**.

In Argentina and Uruguay, you say **¡Hola!**

And in Mexico, it's **Bueno**.

hispanic world

A You have used the word **Cuál** to form different questions. Can you remember how to ask someone for his or her phone number? Work in groups and ask each other for your phone numbers.

B Listen to the numbers that are called out and tick the ones you hear on the bingo card.

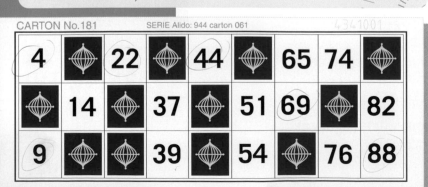

CARTON No.181   SERIE Alido: 944 carton 061   4341001

4		22		44		65	74	
	14		37		51	69		82
9			39		54		76	88

C Listen again and write the numbers that don't appear on the bingo card.

( ) ( ) ( ) ( ) ( )

6 ¿Cuántos años tienes / tiene?

LANGUAGE FOCUS

Tener is an irregular verb and does not follow the normal pattern.

(yo)	**tengo**	*I have*
(tú)	**tie**nes	*you have* (informal)
(usted)	**tie**ne	*you have* (formal)
(él)	**tie**ne	*he has*
(ella)	**tie**ne	*she has*

A Look at the photo and guess the ages of the people. Write them in the first column of the chart on page 24.

Check with your partner by asking:

¿Cuántos años tiene (Ricardo)?

(Ricardo) tiene ( ) años.

Age

To say how old you are in Spanish, use **tener** (to have).

¿Cuántos años tienes? = *How old are you?* (informal)

¿Cuántos años tiene? = *How old are you?* (formal) / *How old is he/she?*

(Literally, *How many years do you / does he/she have?*)

To answer, you use **Tengo** + your age + **años**.

Tengo quince años. = *I am 15.* (literally, *I have 15 years*)

María

Ricardo

Lara

Adso   Guillermo

Name	Guessed age	Correct age
Ricardo		
María		
Guillermo		
Adso		

B Listen to the recording and check how many you got right. Write the correct ages in the second column.

C Fill in the gaps with the right verbs from the box.

me llamo	trabajo
estudio hablo vivo
soy (x 3) te llamas
haces eres (x 2) es
hablas vives (x 2)

Lynn: Hola, buenos días.

Friend: Hola, buenos días. ¿Qué tal?

Lynn: Bien, ¿y usted?

Friend: Bien, pero tutéame.

Lynn: Sí, perdón, ¿y tú?

Friend: ¿Cómo (te llamas)?

Lynn: Lynn. ¿Y usted?

Friend: ¿Perdón?

Lynn: ¿Y tú?

Friend: (me llamo) Ramón Lombardero. ¿ ( ) estadounidense?

Lynn: Sí, ( ) estadounidense, de California. ¿Y tú? ¿De dónde ( )?

Friend: (Soy) mexicano, de Guadalajara ¿Qué (haces)?

Lynn: ( ) enfermera, ( ) en un hospital, pero ahora ( ) español en la universidad de México.

Friend: ¿Qué lenguas (hablas)?

Lynn: (hablo) inglés y un poco de español. Y tú, ¿hablas inglés?

Friend: Sí, y francés también. ¿Y dónde ( )?

Lynn: ( ) en la residencia universitaria "La Salle", en Ciudad de México. ¿(Vives) en la residencia universitaria también?

Friend: Sí, en el Bloque 15. ¿Cuál (es) tu número de teléfono?

Lynn: No tengo teléfono. ¿Y tú?

Friend: Sí, es el 57 28 15 36.

Now listen to the recording and check your answers.

LEARNING TIP:
Tutéame

Spanish speakers use **tutéame** when they want to be informal. It means 'Please use the **tú** form with me'.

también = also

D 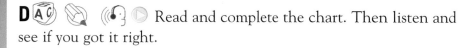 Read and complete the chart. Then listen and see if you got it right.

- Guillermo es cubano.
- El argentino es contable.
- La señora es directora, habla español y francés.
- El cubano es taxista y habla inglés y español.
- La directora tiene 35 años y vive en Bogotá. Es colombiana.
- Julio es argentino, pero vive en Madrid. Tiene 40 años.
- El taxista tiene 49 años y vive en Nueva York.
- El contable habla español e italiano.
- La colombiana se llama Luisa.

Nombre	Nacionalidad	Vive en...	Profesión	Lenguas	Edad

Check that you can...

- use numbers up to 99
- say your phone number in Spanish
- ask for someone else's phone number
- say how old you are
- ask and say how old someone else is

Play the profession game on www.accesslanguages.com.

UNIT **2**

25

Descubre el mundo HISPANO

Francia

Galicia
Asturias
Cantabria
País Vasco
Navarra
La Rioja
Castilla y León
Aragón
Cataluña

Madrid

Portugal

Extremadura

España

Castilla-La Mancha

Valencia

Islas Baleares

Murcia

Andalucía

Islas Canarias

The languages of Spain

Sometimes you will hear the word **castellano** or 'Castilian Spanish' instead of **español**. **El castellano** originated from the language spoken in the Spanish region of Castile (**Castilla**) in the centre of Spain. It is called a 'Romance' language because it originated from Vulgar Latin, the spoken language of the Roman conquerors of Spain. There are three other official languages spoken in Spain alongside **castellano**: **catalán** (in **Cataluña**), **gallego** (in **Galicia**) and **vascuence** (or **euskera**) (in the **País Vasco**, or Basque Country). **Catalán** and **gallego** are also Romance languages.

A Ⓐ Ⓒ Which regions have their own languages? Indicate the different regions and their languages on the map.

B   Read the information about Spain on the web page, then say in English what each of the following details represents.

1	Madrid	**6**	península Ibérica
2	12 de octubre	**7**	39.181.114
3	€	**8**	monarquía constitucional
4	castellano	**9**	99%
5	504.750 km^2	**10**	2%

AOL - [España : Guía completa]

guiadelmundo.com

¿SON ESTOS LOS VALORES QUE QUEREMOS TRANSMITIR A LOS JÓVENES?

Bienvenido
Guia local
España
Mapa
Locución
Himno nacional
Introduccion
Datos Básicos
Historia
Poblacion
Turismo
Hoteles
Postales
Foros
Provincias
Videos
Parajes
Gastronomia
M. Ambiente
Política

CIRCUITOS   VACACIONES   HOTELES   COCHES

– Nombre oficial: Reino de España
– Nombre común: España
– Capital: Madrid
– Continente: Europa
– Situación: Suroeste de Europa, en la península Ibérica, que incluye además las islas Baleares y el archipiélago de Canarias
– Superficie total: 504.750 km^2
– Población: 39.887.150 habitantes
– Religiones: Católicos 99 %, otras religiones 1 %
– Lenguas: La lengua oficial es el español o castellano.

Otras lenguas catalán 17 %, gallego 7%, euskera 2 %
– Fiesta nacional: Día Nacional: 12 de octubre, Constitución: 6 de diciembre
– Forma de gobierno: España es una monarquía constitucional
– Situación Política: Es miembro de la Unión Europea, así como de La ONU y de La OTAN
– Moneda: el Euro €
– Renta per capita: $14.300

Otra gente y yo UNIT **2**

GLOSSARY

Nouns

abogado/a (m/f)	lawyer
año (m)	year
Argentina	Argentina
bar (m)	bar
Bolivia	Bolivia
Brasil	Brazil
camarero/a (m/f)	waiter/waitress
Canadá	Canada
cantante (m/f)	singer
castellano (m)	(Castilian) Spanish
catalán (m)	Catalán (language)
clínica (f)	clinic, surgery
colegio (m)	school
contable (m)	accountant
Cuba	Cuba
director(a) (m/f)	director
enfermero/a (m/f)	nurse
Filipinas	the Philippines
Francia	France
hospital (m)	hospital
Italia	Italy
Japón	Japan
médico (m)	doctor
oficina (f)	office
oficinista (m/f)	office worker, clerk
recepción (f)	reception
recepcionista (m/f)	receptionist
Rusia	Russia
secretario/a (m/f)	secretary
taxista (m/f)	taxi driver
tribunal (m)	lawyer's office
vascuence (m)	Basque (language)

Adjectives

argentino/a	Argentinian
boliviano/a	Bolivian
brasileño/a	Brazilian
canadiense	Canadian
castellano/a	Castilian
catalán/catalana	Catalan
chino/a	Chinese
colombiano/a	Colombian
cubano/a	Cuban
filipino/a	Philippine, Filipino
gallego/a	Galician
japonés/japonesa	Japanese
mexicano/a	Mexican
portugués/portuguesa	Portuguese
ruso/a	Russian

Verbs

hablar	to talk, speak
tener	to have
trabajar	to work
tutear	to call someone **tú**

GLOSSARY

 # LOOKING FORWARD

In **Unit 3**, we will be talking about how to introduce people and family, as well as describing a person's character and appearance.

To prepare, look at the family members listed below.

la familia	family	el hermano	brother
el padre	father	la hermana	sister
la madre	mother	el marido	husband
el hijo	son	la mujer	wife (Sp)
la hija	daughter	la esposa	wife (LA)

UNIT 3
Mi familia y mis amigos

UNIT **2**

UNIT 3
Mi familia y mis amigos

1 ¿Qué recuerdas?

A 🎲 ▷ You are Carmen and you are attending a job interview. Read the CV on the opposite page and answer the questions.

1	¿Cuál es su apellido?	5	¿De dónde es?
2	¿Dónde vive?	6	¿Cuál es su número de teléfono?
3	¿Cuántos años tiene?	7	¿Qué lenguas habla?
4	¿Qué hace?	8	¿Dónde trabaja?

ACCESS SPANISH

DATOS PERSONALES

Nombre: Carmen López Tello
Dirección: C/ Seis de Junio, 9, Valdepeñas (C. Real), España
Teléfono: 926 31 21 49
Dirección electrónica: clopez@lberomail.com
Fecha de nacimiento: 03.12.1980
Nacionalidad: española

EXPERIENCIA PROFESIONAL

Desde 2003   Periodista. **El Canfali**, Ciudad Real

ESTUDIOS

1998–2002   Periodismo. Universidad Complutense de Madrid.

OTROS CONOCIMIENTOS

Idiomas: Español e inglés
Informática: Windows: Word y Excel

LEARNING TIP:

In Spain and Latin-American countries, people have two surnames. The first is their father's first surname and the second is their mother's first surname.

So Carmen **López Tello's** father is Ramón **López** Lombardero, and her mother is María **Tello** Peñasco.

In many countries, when women get married, they take their husband's first surname as a second surname instead of their mother's name, e.g. Carmen's mother could be María **Tello de López**.

In some countries, the second surname is shortened, e.g. Carmen López **T**.

B Now listen and check your answers.

Mi familia y mis amigos UNIT 3

31

2 Mi familia

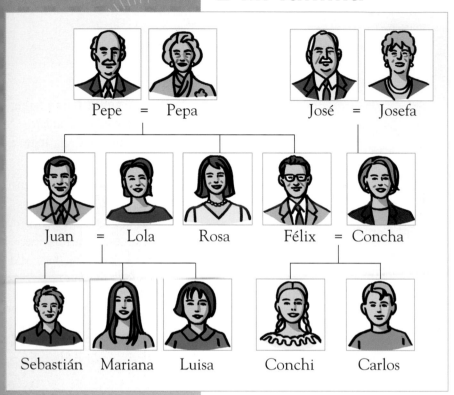

A 🎲🔊⏵ Look at the family tree and complete these sentences. If you're not sure of the words, look back at page 29. Check your answers.

1 La hermana de Mariana se llama ⬭ .

2 Mariana es la ⬭ de Juan y Lola.

3 Concha es la ⬭ de Carlos.

4 Sebastián es el ⬭ de Juan.

5 Carlos es el ⬭ de Conchi.

6 Juan es el ⬭ de Lola.

B 🎲⏵ Look at the family tree again and match the words in **bold** with their meanings.

1 Rosa es **la tía** de Sebastián.   **a** grandfather

2 Sebastián es **el sobrino** de Rosa.   **b** grandmother

3 Conchi es **la prima** de Sebastián.   **c** grandson

4 Sebastián es **el primo** de Conchi.   **d** granddaughter

5 Félix es **el tío** de Luisa.   **e** uncle

6 Luisa es **la sobrina** de Félix.   **f** aunt

7 Pepe es **el abuelo** de Mariana.   **g** nephew

8 Mariana es **la nieta** de Pepe.   **h** niece

9 Josefa es **la abuela** de Carlos.   **i** cousin (male)

10 Carlos es **el nieto** de Josefa.   **j** cousin (female)

It's fun to look at websites of Spanish family trees and histories. Check out the links on www.accesslanguages.com.

C 🎲 ▷ See if you can find the names of ten members of the family.

P	P	R	O	L	D	O	U	D	N
R	H	I	K	O	E	V	X	F	I
I	T	Z	P	J	A	O	O	Y	E
M	Q	H	O	L	D	N	H	W	T
O	M	W	E	I	I	C	N	M	O
H	L	U	R	R	M	K	C	A	X
U	B	A	B	H	M	U	C	D	G
A	M	O	M	N	I	A	J	R	N
I	S	P	U	E	O	J	N	E	N
F	N	C	D	L	L	F	O	O	R

D ✏️ ▷ How many male relationships have you found? Can you change them into female?

How many female relationships have you found? Can you change them into male?

LEARNING TIP:
Masculine plural

In Spanish, the masculine plural also refers to groups containing both sexes.

El príncipe Guillermo tiene cinco primos.

*Prince William has five cousins.**

* on his father's side

The masculine plural form (**primos**) is used, even though four of his cousins are girls.

So **tíos** can mean *uncles* or *aunts and uncles*, and **hijos** can mean *sons* or *sons and daughters* (= *children*). **Hijas** is only used if they are all girls.

¿Cuántos?

You have already come across the question word **¿Cuántos?** meaning *how many* in the expression **¿Cuántos años tiene(s)?**

¿Cuántos? can also be used to ask about other 'quantities'.

¿Cuántos hermanos tienes?
How many brothers (and sisters) have you got?

🎧 LANGUAGE FOCUS

¿Estás casado?

You already know how to ask questions just by adding question marks:

Hablas alemán.   *You speak German.*
¿Hablas alemán?   *Do you speak German?*

In the same way, you can ask someone if he or she is single or married by saying:

¿Estás casado/a?   *Are you married?*
¿Estás soltero/a?   *Are you single?*

You can ask *Do you have any brothers and sisters?* just by saying:

¿Tienes hermanos?

Mi familia y mis amigos UNIT **3**

33

E How would you ask the following questions?

1 Have you got any cousins?

2 Have you got any uncles and aunts?

3 Have you got any children?

4 Are you divorced (**divorciado/a**)?

Can you ask the same questions in a more formal way?

Now can you answer the questions?

F Can you rewrite the questions from activity 2E using **cuántos**?

3 ¿Tenéis hijos?

A Marina is talking about her family. Look at the verbs in the Language Focus and fill in the gaps. Remember to check the subject each time so that you know which part of the verb to use.

Hola, me llamo Marina y voy a hablar de mi familia: Mis padres *(se llaman)* Juan y Carmen, ( ) un hermano que ( ) Guillermo. Guillermo y yo ( ) nueve primos. Mis tíos y mi padre ( ) en un garage, ( ) mecánicos. Todos ( ) en Gerona, y ( ) castellano y catalán. Tambien tengo un perro, se llama Kiko. Y vosotros, ¿ ( ) una familia grande (big)?

Listen and check your answer.

LANGUAGE FOCUS

Ser and *estar*

Ser and **estar** both mean *to be*, but are used in different ways.

To say your name, nationality, profession and to describe yourself or someone else, use the verb **ser**.

yo	**soy**	*I am*	nosotros/as	**somos**	*we are*
tú	**eres**	*you are*	vosotros/as	**sois**	*you are*
usted	**es**	*you are*	ustedes	**son**	*you are*
él/ella	**es**	*he/she is*	ellos/ellas	**son**	*they are*

To say you are single, married, divorced, widowed, etc. or to ask *How are you?*, use the verb **estar**.

yo	**estoy**	*I am*	nosotros/as	**estamos**	*we are*
tú	**estás**	*you are*	vosotros/as	**estáis**	*you are*
usted	**está**	*you are*	ustedes	**están**	*you are*
él/ella	**está**	*he/she is*	ellos/ellas	**están**	*they are*

Verbos plurales

	tener	*to have*	**vivir**	*to live*
nosotros/as	ten**emos**	*we have*	viv**imos**	*we live*
vosotros/as	ten**éis**	*you have*	viv**ís**	*you live*
ustedes	tien**en**	*you have*	viv**en**	*you live*
ellos/ellas	tien**en**	*they have*	viv**en**	*they live*

	trabajar	*to work*	**hablar**	*to speak*
nosotros/as	trabaj**amos**	*we work*	habl**amos**	*we speak*
vosotros/as	trabaj**áis**	*you work*	habl**áis**	*you speak*
ustedes	trabaj**an**	*you work*	habl**an**	*you speak*
ellos/ellas	trabaj**an**	*they work*	habl**an**	*they speak*

Mi familia y mis amigos

UNIT **3**

LANGUAGE FOCUS

La formación del plural

- Adjectives and nouns ending in a vowel: add an –s
  primo**s**   *cousins*
- For most adjectives and nouns ending in a consonant, add –**es**
  español**es**   *Spanish people*

El artículo definido

The article *the* is translated into Spanish by **el**, **la**, **los** or **las**, depending on whether the noun is masculine or feminine, singular or plural.

	masculine	feminine
singular	**el** primo	**la** prima
plural	**los** primos	**las** primas

El caldero

B Change these words into the plural.

1 el abuelo   **2** el tío   **3** el amigo   **4** el actor   **5** el primo   **6** la mujer

C Listen to the conversation and answer the questions in Spanish. Write full sentences.

1 What do Laura and Manuel do for a living?
Laura y Manuel son camareros, trabajan en el restaurante "El caldero".

2 How many children do they have?

3 What are the children called?

4 What do they do?

5 Where do they live?

Presentaciones

éste/ésta *this*

When introducing someone, say:

For a girl or woman: **Ésta es** Carmen.

For a boy or man: **Éste es** Juan.

To say *Pleased to meet you*:

Encantado. (spoken by a man)

Encantada. (spoken by a woman)

Mucho gusto.

éstos/éstas *these*

For more than one person, say:

Éstos son Carlos y Andrés.

Éstos son Marco y Adriana.

Éstas son Carmen y Ana.

D Can you introduce the person sitting on your left to the one on your right?

Now introduce them both to other members of the class.

E Guillermo is introducing his family. Fill in the gaps with **éste**, **ésta**, **éstos** or **éstas**.

Te presento a mi familia. (1) ⬭ es mi padre, Juan. Y (2) ⬭ es mi madre, Carmen. (3) ⬭ es mi hermana, Marina. (4) ⬭ son mis tíos, Ramón, Ignacio y José. Y (5) ⬭ son mis tías, Ana, Pilar y Rosario. Y finalmente (6) ⬭ son mis primos y primas, se llaman Jaime, Rafael, Enrique, Miguel, Ana, Blanca y Raquel.

Now listen and check your answers.

Mi familia y mis amigos UNIT 3

LANGUAGE FOCUS

The following words are used to describe possession:

mi	my	**mi** libro = *my book*
mis	my	**mis** libros = *my books*
tu	your	**tu** libro = *your book*
tus	your	**tus** libros = *your books*
su	his/her/its	**su** libro = *his/her book / your book* (**usted**)
sus	his/her/its	**sus** libros = *his/her books / your books* (**usted**)

To introduce a member of your family, say:

Ésta es **mi** madre.   Éstos son **mis** hermanos.
Éste es **mi** hijo.

But if you are introducing a member of somebody else's family, say:

Éste es **su** hermano.
Éstos son **sus** hermanos.

To ask someone about their family, say:

¿Es ésta **tu** prima?
¿Son éstos **tus** tíos?

LEARNING TIP:

- **Mi**, **tu** and **su** have the same form for masculine and feminine. They are made plural by adding **s** to the singular.

- They must match the number (singular/plural) of the noun they *describe*.

- This is another way to indicate relationships or ownership, using **de** (of):
la hermana **de** mi padre
my father's sister (literally, *the sister of my father*)

el hijo **de** mi prima
my cousin's son (literally, *the son of my cousin*)

4 Mi madre, tus hermanos

A Complete the sentences using the correct forms of the words in brackets.

1 Los hijos de *mis* tíos son *mis* primos. (*my*)

2 El padre de ( ) padre es ( ) abuelo. (*my*)

3 La mujer de ( ) padre es ( ) madre. (*your*)

4 Las hermanas de ( ) padre son ( ) tías. (*his*)

5 Los hijos de ( ) hermano son ( ) sobrinos. (*her*)

6 El abuelo de ( ) primo es ( ) abuelo. (*his*)

7 *Ésta* es la hermana de ( ) madre, ( ) tía. (*your*)

8 ( ) es el padre de ( ) sobrina, ( ) hermano. (*my*)

9 ( ) es el marido de ( ) madre, ( ) padre. (*her*)

10 ( ) es la mujer de ( ) tío, ( ) tía. (*her*)

11 ( ) son los hermanos de ( ) prima, ( ) primos. *(my)*

12 ( ) son los primos de ( ) hermanos, ( ) primos. *(his)*

B  Listen to Juan Carlos introducing his family, then fill in the gaps in the text (look at the family tree to help you).

LEARNING TIP:
Note that **y** (*and*) changes to **e** before a word beginning with **i** or **h**.

Elena **y** Cristina

Jaime **e** Ignacio

Padre **e** hijo

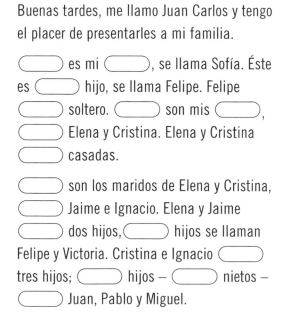

Juan – Sofía

Felipe

Elena – Jaime

Cristina – Ignacio

Felipe Victoria

Juan Pablo Miguel

Buenas tardes, me llamo Juan Carlos y tengo el placer de presentarles a mi familia.

( ) es mi ( ), se llama Sofía. Éste es ( ) hijo, se llama Felipe. Felipe ( ) soltero. ( ) son mis ( ), Elena y Cristina. Elena y Cristina ( ) casadas.

( ) son los maridos de Elena y Cristina, ( ) Jaime e Ignacio. Elena y Jaime ( ) dos hijos, ( ) hijos se llaman Felipe y Victoria. Cristina e Ignacio ( ) tres hijos; ( ) hijos – ( ) nietos – ( ) Juan, Pablo y Miguel.

READY TO MOVE ON?

✓

Check that you can...

- talk about yourself and your family
- ask someone about their family
- use the plural of nouns and verbs
- understand the difference between *ser* and *estar*
- introduce people
- indicate ownership and possession

Mi familia y mis amigos UNIT **3**

5 Las características físicas: ¿Cómo eres?

A 🎲 🔘 Look at the picture and try to guess the meaning of these descriptions.

1 Caperucita es pequeña.

2 Caperucita es guapa.

3 Caperucita y la abuela son delgadas.

4 El cazador (*the hunter*) es alto.

5 El cazador es fuerte.

6 El lobo (*the wolf*) es feo.

7 El lobo es gordo.

8 La abuela es vieja.

9 El cazador y el lobo son grandes.

LEARNING TIP:
Many fairy tales are the same in English and Spanish, but their Spanish names are different:

Caperucita (Roja)   Little Red Riding Hood

La Cenicienta   Cinderella

Blancanieves   Snow White

You will find more practice using Spanish genders at www.accesslanguages.com

B ✏️ 🔘 Now fill in the gaps using adjectives from activity 5A. Follow the general rules for the feminine and plural forms of the adjectives (see pages 19 and 36).

1 El cazador es grande, ⬭ , moreno y ⬭ .

2 Caperucita es rubia, ⬭ y ⬭ .

3 La abuela es ⬭ , baja y ⬭ .

4 El lobo es ⬭ y ⬭ .

Spanish speakers use the word **gafas** for *glasses* (**llevar gafas** = *to wear glasses*). But in Argentina, they use the word **anteojos**; in Mexico, it's **lentes** and in Cuba, **espejuelos**.

Other descriptive words which can change in different countries are:

blonde	rubio/a (Spain)	canche (Central America)
	güero/a (Central America, Mexico)	catiro/a (Colombia and Venezuela)
brown/dark	moreno (Spain)	
	trigueño (other Spanish-speaking countries)	

LANGUAGE FOCUS

Ser y tener

In general, the verb **ser** is used to describe people:
Carlos **es** joven y rubio.
Su abuelo **es** viejo, moreno y calvo.

However, the verb **tener** is used to talk about hair (**pelo**) or eyes (**ojos**).

Rubios claros   Rubios medios   Castaños   Rojos   Negros

ser	tener el pelo	tener el pelo	tener los ojos	tener los ojos	llevar/tener
rubio/a (blonde)	rubio	liso (straight)	negros (black)	grandes (big)	gafas (glasses)
moreno/a (dark)	moreno / negro	rizado (curly)	azules (blue)	pequeños (small)	barba (beard)
castaño/a (chestnut)	castaño	corto (short)	verdes (green)		bigote (moustache)
pelirrojo (red-haired)	rojo	largo (long)	marrones (brown)		
calvo/a (bald)	canoso / gris (grey)		grises (grey)		

UNIT **3**

1

2

3

4

5

6

C 🎲 ▷ Match these famous people with their descriptions.

1 Arnold Schwarzenegger   **4** Kylie Minogue

2 Jennifer Aniston   **5** Penélope Cruz

3 Tom Cruise   **6** Denzel Washington

a Es baja, rubia, delgada, tiene el pelo rizado y largo, es muy guapa.

b Es bajo, moreno, delgado, tiene los ojos verdes y el pelo corto.

c Es alta, rubia, delgada, tiene el pelo largo y liso y los ojos azules.

d Es grande, alto, tiene el pelo corto y castaño.

e Es alto, moreno, pelo corto y rizado, tiene los ojos marrones, es muy guapo.

f Es pequeña y delgada, tiene el pelo negro, largo y liso. Sus ojos son grandes y negros.

D 👂 ▷ Listen to the recording and write the opposite of each word you hear.

E 🗣 👥 ▷ Describe another famous person for the rest of the class to guess.

F ✏️ ▷ Describe the three characters from Little Red Riding Hood without looking at the pictures.

6   La personalidad: ¿Cómo eres?

A 🎲 🎧 ▶ See if you can match the adjectives with their opposites.

1	simpático	**8**	sensible	**a**	tacaño	**h**	perezoso
2	bueno	**9**	tranquilo	**b**	rico	**i**	insensible
3	generoso	**10**	responsable	**c**	antipático	**j**	nervioso
4	trabajador	**11**	fuerte	**d**	tonto	**k**	irresponsable
5	pobre	**12**	optimista	**e**	malo	**l**	débil
6	sincero	**13**	listo	**f**	tímido	**m**	pesimista
7	extrovertido	**14**	inteligente	**g**	mentiroso	**n**	estúpido

Now listen to the recording and check your answers.

B 🎧 ▶ Listen and match the girls with the three boys below.

1 Ana   **2** Luisa   **3** Diana

BUSCANDO. . .

Hola, me llamo Luis Alberto, soy simpático y responsable.

Hola, yo soy Enrique, soy tímido algo perezoso pero soy muy sincero.

Hola, soy Carlos, soy inteligente, sincero y muy trabajador.

LEARNING TIP:
simpático

There is no one English word for **simpático**. It can mean *warm, friendly, funny*, etc. In the dictionary, it is usually translated as *nice*, but this does not cover all of its meanings.

sensible

Be careful of this word – it is a false friend! It looks like the English word *sensible*, but actually means *sensitive*.

44

C 🎲 🎧 ▷ Read this letter and answer the questions in English.

1 What information is given about the writer?

2 How does she describe her father?

3 What negative descriptions does the letter contain?

4 What is good about the writer's sister?

5 What type of person is the writer?

> ¡Hola!
>
> Me llamo Estela, soy venezolana, de Maracaibo, pero vivo en Caracas con mi padre y mi hermana. Tengo 19 años. Mis padres están divorciados.
>
> Mi padre es bajo y moreno, tiene el pelo negro corto y muy liso, los ojos verdes, tiene bigote y barba un poco canosa, trabaja en Correos, es cartero. Es simpático, optimista y trabajador, pero un poco tacaño.
>
> Mi hermana es alta, delgada y pelirroja, tiene muchas pecas, tiene los ojos marrones, es azafata, trabaja en un aeropuerto. Es muy seria y aburrida, pero muy generosa. Habla inglés y francés.
>
> Y yo soy muy tímida y estudiosa, a veces llevo gafas, tengo los ojos pequeños pero muy alegres. Soy bastante alta y delgada, tengo el pelo rojo largo y rizado, los ojos marrones.
>
> Aquí tienes mi foto, escríbeme pronto.
>
> Un abrazo. Estela

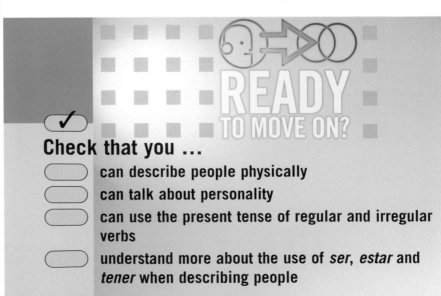

D ✏️ ▷ Now write a letter to a new friend (**amigo/a**) describing yourself and one or two other members of your family.

LEARNING TIP:

Don't panic if you come across words you don't understand in a text. See if you can work out what they mean from the context. For example, can you say what the following words from the letter mean? (Answers below.)

cartero   pecas   azafata

Which two relate to jobs? Which relates to appearance?

azafata = flight attendant
pecas = freckles
cartero = postman

READY TO MOVE ON?

✓

Check that you ...

- can describe people physically
- can talk about personality
- can use the present tense of regular and irregular verbs
- understand more about the use of *ser*, *estar* and *tener* when describing people

AOL - [VENEZUELA]

la máxima autoridad ejecutiva la representa el gobernador y en el caso de los municipios , por el alcalde.

VENEZUELA | Geografía | Recursos naturales | Población | Tradiciones | Símbolos | Símbolos nacionales | Guayana única | La belleza Venezolana

LA VERDADERA REVOLUCIÓN
LA DEBEMOS EMPRENDER EN LA
EDUCACIÓN Y EL TRABAJO

Monumento a Carabobo

La belleza de la mujer venezolana
Miss Mérida 1999

Bellos esteros venezolanos

venepolitica@latinmail.com

Pulse arriba

Latin Beauty

Beauty contests are very important for national prestige in Latin American countries. Since the creation of Miss Universe in 1952, seventeen of the winners have been from Latin America: four Venezuelans, four Puerto Ricans and winners from Peru, Colombia, Argentina, Mexico, Chile and Panama. There have also been five Venezuelan Miss World title holders, along with winners from Argentina, Peru, Puerto Rico and the Dominican Republic. Venezuelans Irene Sáez and Bárbara Palacios are ex-beauty queens whose success has led to professional careers in the USA. Bárbara Palacios runs a successful jewellery business in Miami. Irene Sáez became a mayor and a governor, as well a candidate for the presidency of the republic of Venezuela, and now works for the Colonial Bank of South Florida. She won the Miss Universe contest in 1981 and at the time was considered one of the most beautiful women in history. But the Venezuelans' reputation was further enhanced when she found herself competing in the same year with a Miss World also from Venezuela: this was the first time in history that both title holders had come from the same country.

A Read the article about *Latin Beauty* and say whether the statements below are true (**verdadero**) or false (**falso**).

1 Cinco venezolanas han obtenido el título de Miss Universo.

2 Hay más venezolanas con el título de Miss Mundo que argentinas.

3 Irene Sáez compitió con Bárbara Palacios por el título de Miss Universo.

4 Bárbara Palacios nunca obtuvo el título de Miss Universo.

5 Irene Sáez trabaja en un banco ahora.

B Listen to the interview with Irene Sáez. Note down the information you hear, then write a description of real Venezuelan women.

LEARNING TIP:

broma = *joke*

nunca = *never*

ahora = *now*

3

45

GLOSSARY

Nouns

abuela (f)	grandmother
abuelo (m)	grandfather
amigo/a (m/f)	friend
barba (f)	beard
bigote (m)	moustache
familia (f)	family
hermana (f)	sister
hermano (m)	brother
hija (f)	daughter
hijo (m)	son
hijos (mpl)	children
gafas (fpl)	glasses
madre (f)	mother
marido (m)	husband
mujer (f)	woman, wife
nieta (f)	granddaughter
nieto (m)	grandson
padre (m)	father
prima (f)	(female) cousin
primo (m)	(male) cousin
sobrina (f)	niece
sobrino (m)	nephew
tía (f)	aunt
tío (m)	uncle

Adjectives

alto/a	tall
antipático/a	unkind, nasty
azul	blue
bajo/a	short (height)
bueno/a	good
calvo/a	bald
canoso/a	grey(-haired)
casado/a	married
castaño/a	chestnut
corto/a	short (length)
débil	weak
delgado/a	slim
divorciado/a	divorced
extrovertido/a	outgoing
feo/a	ugly
fuerte	strong
generoso/a	generous
gordo/a	fat
grande	big
gris	grey
guapo/a	pretty, good-looking
insensible	insensitive
irresponsable	irresponsible
largo/a	long
liso/a	straight
listo/a	clever
malo/a	bad
marrón/marrones	brown
mentiroso/a	lying, liar
mi	my
moreno/a	dark
negro/a	black
nervioso/a	nervous
optimista	optimistic
pelirrojo/a	red-haired

GLOSSARY

pequeño/a	small	tonto/a	stupid
perezoso/a	lazy	trabajador(a)	hard-working
pesimista	pessimistic	tranquilo/a	calm
pobre	poor	verde	green
responsable	responsible	viudo/a	widowed
rico/a	rich		
rizado/a	curly	**Verbs**	
rojo/a	red	estar	to be
rubio/a	blonde, fair		
sensible	sensitive	**Others**	
simpático/a	nice, kind	ésta (f)	this
sincero/a	sincere, honest	éste (m)	this
soltero/a	single		
su	his/her/its	**Expressions**	
	your/their/yours	a veces	sometimes
tacaño/a	mean, stingy	Mucho gusto.	Pleased to meet you.
tímido/a	shy		

LOOKING FORWARD

In **Unit 4**, we will look at shopping for food and clothes. Look at the following words. Which do you think are words for food and which are words for clothes?

agua • blusa • camisa • carne • chaqueta • falda • fruta • galletas • jamón jersey • leche • manzana • naranja • pan • pantalón • pescado • plátano queso • zapatos

UNIT 4
¿Qué desea?

UNIT 4
¿Qué desea?

By the end of this unit you will be able to:

- Ask for items in a shop
- Talk about types of shops and products
- Ask and talk about weight, quality, colour, sizes
- Describe things
- Understand prices

1 ¿Qué recuerdas?

A Read the article about Juan, which appeared in a local Spanish magazine. Say whether the following statements are **verdadero** (*true*), **falso** (*false*) or **no se sabe** (*don't know*).

1 Juan is a painter from Guadalupe.

2 Juan is nice, hard working, optimistic and outgoing.

3 He is married with two children.

4 His brothers are models, and his sister is an engineer.

5 His wife is tall, blonde and pretty.

6 His sister is small and fat, with black hair and brown eyes.

ACCESS SPANISH

Juan Fernández, ganador del concurso Frida Kahlo

Juan es pintor. Es mexicano, de Guadalupe. Tiene cuarenta años, es simpático, optimista, trabajador y muy extrovertido. Está casado con Paula que es estadounidense, de Dallas. Es diseñadora. Tienen dos hijos: Carlos, su hijo, tiene doce años y Eva, su hija, tiene diez. Sus hermanos se llaman José y Luis Fernando, son ingenieros, y Carmen, su hermana, es modelo. Carmen es morena, alta y delgada, tiene los ojos marrones y el pelo negro y rizado, es muy guapa. Está soltera y vive con Juan, Paula y sus hijos.

Juan Fernández, ganador

Juan Fernández, ganador del concurso Frida Kahlo

B Rewrite the article as though you are Juan. Don't forget to change the verbs and pronouns to agree with the subject.

(Yo) soy pintor …

C Read the article about Oxana Fedorova and try to get the general idea. Can you describe her in English? What is she doing now?

Oxana Fedorova (Miss Universo)

Miss Panamá, Justine Pasek, y Miss China, Linz Zhuo, fueron elegidas Primera y Segunda Dama de Honor, respectivamente

Oxana Fedorova, Miss Rusia – 24 años, pelo negro y ojos verdes – es desde anoche Miss Universo 2002 y también la primera mujer rusa que ostenta el título. Su belleza, su estilo, elegancia y personalidad cautivaron a los diez miembros del jurado especialmente tras responder a la última y decisiva pregunta "¿Qué te hace ruborizar?", a lo que ella contestó: "Cuando me equivoco al responder". En Oxana, se conjugan belleza e inteligencia ya que, a sus 24 años, es profesora en la Universidad del Ministerio de Interior de San Petersburgo donde además cursa un postgrado tras concluir su licenciatura en leyes.

Oxana Fedorova

2 En el estanco (At the tobacconist's)

A Listen to the dialogue and, without looking at the text below, try to make a list of the items the customer buys. Remember you don't need to understand every word, but try to recognise the ones you know and get the general idea.

B Now listen to the dialogue again and read the transcript.

Shop assistant:	Buenos días. **¿Qué desea?**
Client:	**¿Cuánto cuestan** las postales?
Shop assistant:	0,25€.
Client:	**Quisiera** dos postales.
Shop assistant:	**¿Algo más?**
Client:	Sí, **¿tiene** sellos?
Shop assistant:	Sí.
Client:	**Quisiera** dos sellos para Estados Unidos.
Shop assistant:	**Aquí tiene, ¿algo más?**
Client:	**Quisiera** un periódico también. **¿Tiene** periódicos norteamericanos?
Shop assistant:	Lo siento, sólo tenemos ingleses, franceses y alemanes.
Client:	Quisiera un periódico inglés. ¿Qué periódicos tiene?
Shop assistant:	*The Times, the Independent, the Sun* y *the Daily Mirror.*
Client:	**¿Tiene** revistas inglesas?
Shop assistant:	No, lo siento, sólo tenemos revistas españolas.
Client:	¡Qué pena!
Shop assistant:	**¿Algo más?**
Client:	No. **¿Cuánto es todo?**
Shop assistant:	Son dos postales 0,50 céntimos y dos sellos para Estados Unidos 1,00€. En total 1,50€.
Client:	Aquí tiene 2€.
Shop assistant:	Su cambio, 50 céntimos. Gracias.
Client:	De nada. Adiós.

C These statements refer to the dialogue on the previous page. Are they **verdadero** (true) or **falso** (false)?

1 The stamps are for the USA.

2 You can buy newspapers from almost any country in Europe and America.

3 The only magazines are Spanish.

4 The client buys an English newspaper.

5 0.50€ is the change from the shopping.

D Look at the dialogue again and match the key phrases (in **bold**) with their English equivalents.

1	¿Qué desea?	**a**	Anything else?
2	¿Cuánto cuesta(n) …?	**b**	Have you got … ?
3	¿Algo más?	**c**	How much is it altogether?
4	Aquí tiene.	**d**	Can I help you?
5	¿Cuánto es todo?	**e**	I would like …
6	Quisiera …	**f**	Here you are.
7	¿Tiene …?	**g**	How much is the … ?

E Look at each list of items and decide which cannot be bought in that shop.

1 En **un estanco** compramos: sellos   sobres   postales   pan

2 En **una papelería** compras: libros   cuadernos   zapatos   bolígrafos

3 En **una farmacia** compro: aspirinas   crema para el sol   vino   tiritas

4 **Una tienda de comestibles** vende: mapas   bebidas   fruta   leche

5 En **los quioscos** venden: revistas   periódicos   vestidos   postales

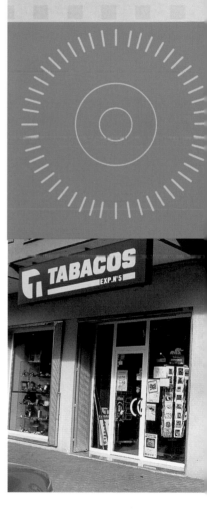

¿Qué desea?

Visit our website for extra practice o
numbers

LANGUAGE FOCUS

Comprar y vender

Comprar (*to buy*) is a regular **–ar** verb.

yo	compr**o**	*I buy*
tú	compr**as**	*you buy*
usted	compr**a**	*you buy*
él/ella	compr**a**	*he/she buys*
nosotros/as	compr**amos**	*we buy*
vosotros/as	compr**áis**	*you buy*
ustedes	compr**an**	*you buy*
ellos/ellas	compr**an**	*they buy*

Vender (*to sell*) is a regular **–er** verb.

vend**o**	*I sell*
vend**es**	*you sell*
vend**e**	*you sell*
vend**e**	*he/she sells*
vend**emos**	*we sell*
vend**éis**	*you sell*
vend**en**	*you sell*
vend**en**	*they sell*

3 Más números

LANGUAGE FOCUS

Los números: 100 →

100   cien

101 to 199 are formed using the word **ciento.**

101	ciento uno
102	ciento dos
123	ciento veintitrés
145	ciento cuarenta y cinco

LEARNING TIP:
Numbers

Note that you don't need to put **uno** in front of **cien**:

cien = *one/a hundred*

Be careful with **quinientos** (500), **setecientos** (700) and **novecientos** (900), which don't follow the normal pattern of adding **cientos** to the number.

200	doscientos

200 to 999 are formed using the suffix **cientos.**

300	trescientos
400	cuatrocientos
500	quinientos
600	seiscientos
700	setecientos
800	ochocientos
900	novecientos
209	doscientos nueve
437	cuatrocientos treinta y siete
568	quinientos sesenta y ocho
715	setecientos quince
925	novecientos veinticinco

A Match the written numbers with the figures.

1	cuatrocientos treinta y cinco		**a**	163
2	seiscientos veinticinco		**b**	435
3	quinientos dos		**c**	398
4	novecientos quince		**d**	625
5	ciento sesenta y tres		**e**	915
6	trescientos noventa y ocho		**f**	502

B Try to say the following numbers.

a 382 **b** 478 **c** 267 **d** 515 **e** 125 **f** 976

Now write them down.

4 La alimentación (Food)

A On the right is a list of goods that you might find in either your fridge or your cupboard. Say what you can see in the fridge (**el frigorífico**) and in the cupboard (**el armario**).

✓

Check that you can...
- ask for items in a shop
- talk about types of shops and products
- buy postcards, stamps and newspapers
- understand prices
- use numbers up to 999

la cerveza, el café, el té, el azúcar, la leche, la fruta, la carne, el pescado, el vino blanco, el vino tinto, el jamón, las galletas, el pan, el queso, el arroz, la mermelada

... en el frigorífico

... en el armario

Go to www.accesslanguages.com to learn more about Spanish shopping on the Internet.

UNIT **4**

53

LANGUAGE FOCUS

Los artículos (*the*)

Look at the following words:

el pollo (*chicken*)   masculine singular
la cerveza (*beer*)   feminine singular
los guisantes (*peas*)   masculine plural
las verduras (*vegetables*)   feminine plural

el, **la**, **los** and **las** all mean *the*. In Spanish, the word for *the* varies according to the gender and the number of the word it refers to. Remember that things as well as people have genders in Spanish.

LEARNING TIP:

Remember that the ends of words can often give you a clue to their gender: words ending in **–o** are usually masculine, words ending in **–a** are usually feminine, and the plural ends in **–s**.

B Imagine that you're showing your friend Michael how to cook a typical Spanish omelette. You need him to pass you various ingredients. Fill in the gaps using **el**, **la**, **los**, **las**.

Michael, pásame … por favor.

1 ( ) pimienta   4 ( ) cebolla

2 ( ) patatas   5 ( ) sal (f)

3 ( ) huevos   6 ( ) aceite (m)

C Listen, look at the panel on page 55 and find out which products are on special offer (**en oferta**).

Carnicería	ternera, cerdo, cordero, pollo
Charcutería	salchichas, jamón
Pescadería	calamares, gambas, mejillones, almejas, bacalao, merluza, salmón, atún
Frutería	naranjas, manzanas, peras, plátanos, pomelos, uvas
Verdura	tomates, pepino, lechuga, pimientos, judías verdes, guisantes, champiñones
Lácteos	leche, mantequilla, queso, yogur

LEARNING TIP:

As with other countries in the European Union, the currency in Spain is **el euro** € (*the euro*), which is divided into 100 **céntimos** (*cents*).

Notice that a comma, not a decimal point, is used between euros and cents (the decimal point is used for thousands, e.g. 3.000€ = tres mil euros = three thousand euros).

There are different ways of saying prices:

3,67€ tres euros, sesenta y siete céntimos

tres euros sesenta y siete

tres sesenta y siete

tres con sesenta y siete

D [A C] Look at the shopping list and match the containers and quantities with the products.

100 gramos		cerveza
un paquete		café
cuatro latas		té
un kilo	**de**	azúcar
una caja		leche
una barra		fruta
una bolsa		carne
dos kilos		pescado
un litro		vino blanco
dos botellas		vino tinto
un bote		jamón
		galletas
		pan
		queso
		arroz
		mermelada

¿Qué desea?
UNIT 4

1 kilo de pollo
½ kilo de gambas
½ kilo de arroz
¼ kilo de calamares
¼ kilo de mejillones
100 gramos de almejas
una lata de guisantes
una bolsa de judias
verdes
dos pimientos
un ajo
una cebolla
una botella de aceite

E 🎲 ▶ Today you want to cook a paella, a typical Spanish dish from Valencia. You make a shopping list, but when you get home, you find that you have forgotten some of the ingredients. Look at the picture. Which ones are missing?

F 🎧 ▶ Listen to the conversation in the grocer's (**la tienda de comestibles**) and answer the questions.

1 Which of the following items *didn't* the customer buy?

- 250 gramos de jamón serrano
- 250 gramos de jamón de York
- ¼ kilo de queso gallego
- dos barras de pan
- una botella de leche
- una lata de atún
- una botella de aceite

2 Did he buy anything else?

3 How much did he pay?

G 👥 🎲 ▶ Think of a typical recipe and prepare a role-play in which your partner buys all the ingredients. The rest of the group has to guess what you are trying to make.

LEARNING TIP:

In Spain, each area has many different food specialities, for example:

- **jamón serrano:** a typical Spanish naturally cured ham. It is different from **jamón de York**, which is cooked like British ham.
- **queso manchego** (originally from la Mancha), **queso de Burgos** (from Burgos), **queso gallego** (from Galicia), etc.
- **embutidos:** different types of cooked or cured sausage like **chorizo** (spicy sausage), **salchichón** (salami), **longaniza**, **lomo**, **morcilla** (black pudding), etc.

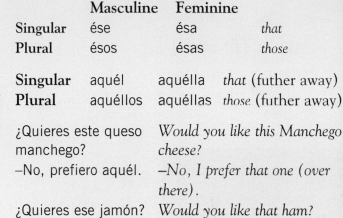

éstos, éstas

In Unit 3, you learned how to use **éste** and **ésta** to introduce people.

They can also be used to specify things. As they have to agree in number as well as gender with the thing they refer to, they have a plural form: **éstos** (masculine plural) and **éstas** (feminine plural).

	Masculine	Feminine	
Singular	éste	ésta	*this*
Plural	éstos	éstas	*these*

Quisiera vino tinto.	*I would like some red wine.*
– ¿Quiere **éste**?	*– Would you like **this one**?*
Vale.	*OK.*

The words for *that (one)* and *those (ones)* work in a similar way.

	Masculine	Feminine	
Singular	ése	ésa	*that*
Plural	ésos	ésas	*those*
Singular	aquél	aquélla	*that* (futher away)
Plural	aquéllos	aquéllas	*those* (futher away)

¿Quieres este queso manchego?	*Would you like this Manchego cheese?*
–No, prefiero aquél.	*–No, I prefer that one (over there).*
¿Quieres ese jamón?	*Would you like that ham?*
–No, prefiero éste.	*–No, I prefer this one.*

Other currencies in Latin America:

hispanic world

- el peso (Mexico, Colombia, Chile, Argentina, Uruguay, Cuba, Dominican Republic)
- el bolívar (Venezuela)
- el sucre (Ecuador)
- el sol (Peru)
- el córdoba (Nicaragua)
- la lempira (Honduras)
- el quetzal (Guatemala)
- el balboa (Panama)
- el colón (Costa Rica, El Salvador)
- el dólar (USA, Puerto Rico)

LEARNING TIP:
éste or *este*?

Este, **ese**, **aquel**, etc. are called 'demonstratives'. When they are used with the noun (as adjectives), they don't have an accent. When they replace the noun (as pronouns), they have the accent.

The accent doesn't affect the way you say the word.

ese and *aquel*

Spanish has two words for *that*: **ese** and **aquel**.
Aquel is used to describe things that are further away from the speaker than **ese**.

Quisiera un plátano.	*I'd like a banana.*
–¿**Ése**?	*–That one?*
No, **aquél**.	*No, that one (over there).*

LANGUAGE FOCUS

querer (*to want*)

quiero	*I want*
¿quieres?	*Do you want?* (informal)
¿quiere?	*Do you want?* (formal)

Note that **quiero** is often translated as *I would like*. It is not as blunt as the English *I want*. You have already come across another way of saying *I would like* in Spanish: **quisiera**.

H You and your friend are in the supermarket discussing which items to buy to make your recipe from activity 4G. Prepare a full role-play, buying everything you need from the different departments. Use the pictures to help you (remember to include the assistant's part).

When they arrived in America, the Spanish Conquistadors came across new kinds of vegetables and fruits which completely changed the European diet. They also introduced changes in the native diet. Here are some Spanish words for items which are different in Latin America.

Castillian	Latin American	English
aguacate	palta	*avocado*
albaricoque	damasco	*apricot*
champiñón	callampa / choclo / hongo / seta	*mushroom*
fresa	frutilla	*strawberry*
judías verdes	ejotes (Mex.) / chauchas (Argent.)	*green beans*
judías	frijoles / porotos	*beans*
maíz	elote (Mex.) / choclo	*corn*
melocotón	durazno	*peach*
patata	papa	*potato*
piña	ananás	*pineapple*
plátano	banana	*banana*
pomelo	toronja	*grapefruit*
tomate	jitomate	*tomato*
zumo	jugo	*juice*
pastel	torta	*cake*

Check that you ...

- can ask for particular items of food
- can talk about departments in a supermarket
- can buy food by weight and/or container
- understand prices
- can use *este*, *ese*, *aquel*, etc.
- can express preferences

UNIT **4**

5 La moda

la bufanda

la camiseta

la chaqueta

la corbata

el abrigo

la blusa

el vestido

los guantes

la camisa

45€

60€

30€

32€

10€

8€

42€

120€

17€

35€

200€

65€

la falda

40€

los zapatos

70€

las zapatillas

100€

los vaqueros

80€

los pantalones

75€

las botas

el traje (chaqueta y pantalon

rojo **azul** amarillo **verde** **negro** blanco

naranja **gris** rosa **marrón** **púrpura**

A Sit back-to-back with a partner and take turns to describe what the other person is wearing.

Mi compañero/a lleva …

B  Imagine that you are going on holiday. What clothes would you pack if you were going to:

1 Spain for a beach holiday?   **3** France for a camping holiday?

2 Austria for a skiing holiday?

Use a dictionary to find words you don't know.

C Listen to the following conversations in a department store and complete the chart.

	Item	Colour wanted	Price	Do they buy it?
Customer 1				
Customer 2				
Customer 3				
Customer 4				

LANGUAGE FOCUS

Lo, la, los, las

In Spanish, as in English, you can avoid repeating a noun by using a pronoun.
The Spanish pronouns are **lo**, **la**, **los** and **las**; as you might expect, they change gender depending on the object referred to:

	Masculine	Feminine	
Singular	lo	la	*it*
Plural	los	las	*them*

Quisiera **un abrigo**. **Lo** quiero negro.
Quisiera **unos pantalones**. **Los** quiero azules.

Quisiera **una camisa**. **La** quiero blanca.
Quisiera **unas botas**. **Las** quiero verdes.

The pronouns usually come before the verb, as in the examples above. But if the verb is an infinitive or imperative (more about this in Unit 6), it is added onto the end of the verb.

Assistant: ¿Qué tal **las botas**? ¿**Las** compra?
   or   ¿Qué tal **las botas**? ¿Va a comprar**las**?
Client: No sé.
Friend: ¡Cómpre**las**! ('*Buy them!*')

de lunares	de cuadros	de rayas/listas	estampado/a/s

Tela (*fabric*)

algodón
(*cotton*)

lana
(*wool*)

seda
(*silk*)

lino
(*linen*)

piel/cuero
(*leather*)

LEARNING TIP:
llevar

Llevar is a very versatile verb.
It can mean:

- to wear
  Lleva unos vaqueros negros.
  He's wearing black jeans.

- to take
  Me los **llevo**.
  I'll take them.

- to carry
  Lleva una bolsa.
  She's carrying a bag.

Opinions

Es caro/barato.
It's expensive/cheap.

Es grande/pequeño.
It's big/small.

Es bonito/feo.
It's pretty/ugly.

Es clásico/moderno.
It's classic/modern.

Es estrecho/ancho.
It's tight/loose.

Es largo/corto.
It's long/short.

vale = OK

D 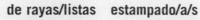 Look at the picture below and fill in the gaps, using the right pronoun where necessary. Then listen to the recording and check your answers.

Shop assistant: Buenas tardes, ¿qué desea?

Client: Quisiera un abrigo.

Shop assistant: ¿Cómo ⬭ quiere?

Client: ⬭ quiero de ⬭ ⬭ ⬭.

Shop assistant: ¿Cuál es su talla?

Client: Es la 40.

Shop assistant: Un momento, aquí ⬭ tiene.

Client: ¿Puedo probárme⬭?

Shop assistant: Sí, naturalmente. ¿Qué tal? ¿Se ⬭ lleva?

Client: No sé, es un poco clásico. ¿Cuánto cuesta?

Shop assistant: Cuesta 130€. ¿Se ⬭ lleva?

Client: Lo siento, no me ⬭ llevo. Es muy caro.

Shop assistant: Éste es más barato.

Client: Es muy clásico. ⬭ quiero más moderno.

Shop assistant: Lo siento, sólo tenemos éstos.

Client: Vale, gracias.

Shop assistant: De nada, adiós.

Client: Adiós.

LANGUAGE FOCUS

cuesta / cuestan, vale / valen

¿Cuánto **cuesta**?
¿Cuánto **cuestan**?
    or

¿Cuánto **vale**?   *How much is it?*
¿Cuánto **valen**?   *How much are they?*

E Look at these pictures. Describe the clothes and give your opinion.

F ¿Qué tipo de ropa te gusta llevar?

1 Look at the web page and describe what the people are wearing.

2 Write a text about your own personal style and explain what kind of clothes you like wearing. Use the following text as a model.

Prefiero ir a la moda, prefiero llevar vaqueros, camisetas de algodón blancas, prefiero el color blanco ...

LEARNING TIP:
Expresiones

ir a la moda	*to be in fashion*
ir de escaparates	*to go window shopping* (Spain)
ir a juego / hacer juego	*to match*
regatear	*to bargain/haggle*
ser una ganga	*to be a bargain*
estar en rebajas	*to be on sale* (Spain)
la liquidación	*Sale* (Lat.Am.)
el escaparate	*shop window* (Spain)
la vitrina	*shop window* (LA)

The Spanish words for items of clothing can vary from one country to another:

coat	abrigo	sobretodo (m), tapado (f) (Arg.)
bag	bolso	cartera (Arg.) / bolsa (Mex.)
jacket	chaqueta	saco
skirt	falda	pollera (Arg.)
sweater	jersey	suéter
sandals	sandalias	huaraches (Mex.)
jeans	vaqueros	tejanos

READY TO MOVE ON?

Check that you can ...

- ask for particular clothing in a shop
- ask and talk about colour, material and sizes of clothing
- understand prices
- use direct object pronouns *lo*, *la*, *los*, *las*

Los diseñadores dominicanos

El carácter dominicano tiene una afinidad natural con la belleza y una tendencia a registrar y expresar visualmente la experiencia de ser dominicano. Y es precisamente la mezcla de lo caribeño con la contemporaneidad lo que les hace creadores de diseños frescos y elegantes. Realmente, existe un aspecto tropical en la manera en la que tratan el color, o una expresividad cultural en el modo en el que diseñan la ropa.

Descubre el mundo HISPANO

Oscar de la Renta

Oscar de la Renta dejó nuestra natal República Dominicana a la edad de 18 años para estudiar pintura en la Academia de San Fernando en Madrid, España. Durante su estadía en esta nación, se interesó en el mundo del diseño y comenzó a realizar diseños para afamadas casas de modas líderes en ese entonces, lo cual le llevó a un aprendizaje con el renombrado "couturier", Cristobal Balenciaga.

Luego Oscar de la Renta dejó España para unirse con Antonio Castillo como asistente en la casa Lanvin en París.

En 1963, Oscar de la Renta partió a New York para diseñar una colección para Elizabeth Arden.

En 1965, el Sr. de la Renta comenzó con su firma [etiqueta de ropa] lista para vestir (ready to wear).

La Firma Oscar de la Renta esta compuesta por la Colección [de ropa] Lista para Vestir y la Pink Label ([etiqueta] Rosada). Para complementar estos diseños, en el Otoño del 2001 fue el debut de los Accesorios Oscar de la Renta; Bultos, correas, joyas, zapatos y bufandas.

A  Read the web page about Oscar de la Renta and answer the questions about his career.

1   When and why did he leave the Dominican Republic?

2   Which famous designers has he worked with?

3   When did he start his own firm?

4   When did he introduce accessories?

5   Which accessories does he have in his collection?

B Five things you should know about the Dominican Republic. Match the words with their descriptions:

1   ámbar, larimar   3   puros   5   cerveza "La Presidente"

2   merengue   4   ron

a   Piedras hermosas que puedes admirar y adquirir en República Dominicana.

b   Cigarros, elaborados a mano, que hoy en día gozan de un enorme prestigio en todo el mundo.

c   Forma habitual de tomarla es a punto de congelación y algunos suelen mezclarla con el jugo de tomates en lata.

d   Es un baile y ritmo contagioso dominicano.

e   En estas tierras se produce uno de los mejores del mundo. Existen diversos tipos que van desde el oscuro, el dorado, el añejo, especial, etc.

Go to our website for more links to sites about the Dominican Republic.

4

GLOSSARY

Nouns

abrigo (m)	coat
aceite (m)	oil
ajo (m)	garlic
algodón (m)	cotton
almejas (fpl)	clams
armario (m)	cupboard
arroz (m)	rice
atún (m)	tuna
azúcar (m)	sugar
bacalao (m)	cod
barra (f)	loaf
bolsa (f)	bag
botas (fpl)	boots
bote (m)	jar
botella (f)	bottle
café (m)	coffee
calamares (mpl)	squid
camisa (f)	shirt
carnicería (f)	butcher's
cebolla (f)	onion
céntimo (m)	cent
cerdo (m)	pork
cerveza (f)	beer
champiñones (mpl)	mushrooms
chaqueta (f)	jacket
charcutería (f)	delicatessen/cold meats
chorizo (m)	spicy sausage
cordero (m)	lamb
cuero (m)	leather
escaparate (m)	shop window
Estados Unidos (mpl)	the United States
estanco (m)	tobacconist's
euro (m)	euro
falda (f)	skirt
farmacia (f)	chemist's
frigorífico (m)	fridge
fruta (f)	fruit
frutería (f)	fruit shop
galletas (fpl)	biscuits
gambas (fpl)	prawns
gramo (m)	gram
guisantes (mpl)	peas
huevo (m)	egg
jamón (m)	ham
jersey (m)	sweater
judías verdes (fpl)	green beans
kilo (m)	kilo
lácteos (mpl)	dairy products
lana (f)	wool
lata (f)	tin, can
leche (f)	milk
lechuga (f)	lettuce
lino (m)	linen
liquidación (f)	sale
litro (m)	litre
mantequilla (f)	butter
manzana (f)	apple
mejillones (mpl)	mussels
merluza (f)	hake
mermelada (f)	jam
naranja (f)	orange
oferta (f)	offer
pan (m)	bread
panadería (f)	baker's
pantalones (mpl)	trousers
papelería (f)	stationer's
paquete (m)	packet

pepino (m)	cucumber	**vino tinto** (m)	red wine
pera (f)	pear	**yogur** (m)	yoghurt
periódico (m)	newspaper		
pescadería (f)	fishmonger's	## Adjectives	
piel (f)	leather, skin	**amarillo/a**	yellow
pimienta (f)	pepper (condiment)	**ancho/a**	loose
pimiento (m)	pepper (vegetable)	**aquel/aquella/aquellos/**	
plátano (m)	banana	**aquellas**	that/those (over there)
pollo (m)	chicken	**azul**	blue
pomelo (m)	grapefruit	**barato/a**	cheap, inexpensive
queso (m)	cheese	**blanco/a**	white
quiosco (m)	kiosk, newspaper stand	**caro/a**	expensive
rebajas (fpl)	sales	**clásico/a**	classical
revista (f)	magazine	**corto/a**	short
sal (f)	salt	**de cuadros**	checked
salchichón (m)	spicy sausage	**de listas**	striped
salmón (m)	salmon	**de lunares**	spotted
sandalias (fpl)	sandals	**de rayas**	striped
seda (f)	silk	**ese/esa/esos/esas**	that/those
talla (f)	size	**estampado/a**	patterned
té (m)	tea	**este/esta/estos/estas**	this/these
tela (f)	material, fabric	**estrecho/a**	tight
ternera (f)	veal	**gris**	grey
tienda de comestibles (f)	grocer's	**marrón**	brown
tienda de moda (f)	clothes shop	**naranja**	orange
tomate (m)	tomato	**negro/a**	black
uvas (fpl)	grapes	**pequeño/a**	small
vaqueros (mpl)	jeans	**púrpura**	purple
verduras (fpl)	vegetables	**rosa**	pink
vino blanco (m)	white wine	**verde**	green

¿Qué desea? UNIT 4

GLOSSARY

Verbs

comprar	to buy
costar (cuesta(n))	to cost
desear	to wish, want
llevar	to wear, take, carry
probar	to try
querer	to want
regatear	to bargain, haggle
vender	to sell

Pronouns

aquél/aquélla/aquéllos/ aquéllas	that/those (over there)
ése/ésa/ésos/ésas	that/those
éste/ésta/éstos/éstas	this/these
lo/la/los/las	it/them

Others

aquí	here
para	for

Expressions

¿Algo más?	Anything else?
¿Cuánto es todo?	How much is it altogether?
cuarto kilo	a quarter of a kilo
estar en rebajas	to be in a sale
hacer juego	to match, go together
ir a juego	to match, go together
ir a la moda	to be fashionable
ir de escaparates	to go window-shopping
medio kilo	half a kilo
Prefiero …	I prefer …
¡Qué pena!	What a shame!
¿Qué desea?	What would you like?
Quisiera …	I would like …
ser una ganga	to be a bargain
Vale.	OK.

LOOKING FORWARD

In **Unit 5**, we will look at menus and how to order food and drink.

To prepare, look at the following menu:

UNIT 5
El restaurante

MENÚ DEL DÍA

Primer plato
Sopa del día
soup of the day

Gazpacho
Guisantes con jamón
peas with ham

Segundo plato
Filete con patatas fritas
steak and chips

Sardinas a la plancha y ensalada mixta
grilled sardines and mixed salad

Paella de la casa
house paella

Pollo asado con pimientos
roast chicken with peppers

Postre
Fruta del tiempo
fruit of the season

Helado
ice cream

Pan y vino
bread and wine

20€

UNIT **4**

UNIT 5
El restaurante

By the end of this unit you will be able to:

- Understand menus
- Order food and drink
- Ask about items on the menu
- Say what food and drink you like and don't like
- Pay compliments
- Accept and decline invitations

1 ¿Qué recuerdas?

A 🎧 A∁ ▷ Where would you hear these conversations?
Choose the right shop.

1 **a** En una panadería. **b** En una carnicería. **c** En un estanco.

2 **a** En un quiosco. **b** En una pescadería. **c** En una boutique.

3 **a** En una frutería. **b** En una tienda de comestibles.
   c En una carnicería.

4 **a** En una tienda de moda. **b** En una farmacia. **c** En una librería.

5 **a** En una pastelería. **b** En una papelería. **c** En una panadería.

ACCESS SPANISH

B Write the dialogue in the correct order.

a
¿Qué desea?
Sí, tenemos vinos de Rioja, Ribera del Duero, Valdepeñas, Ribeiro y Penedés.
Buenos días.
¿Tiene vinos españoles?
Hola, buenos días.

b
No, ése es muy caro.
¿Lo quiere tinto o blanco?
Éste está de oferta, son 20€.
Lo quiero tinto.
¿Cuánto vale el Rioja?

c
No, blanco.
Quisiera una botella de vino tinto.
Sí, otra botella, de Ribeiro.
Vale 10€.
El vino de Valdepeñas es muy bueno y es más barato.
¿Cuánto vale?
¿Lo quiere tinto?
¿Algo más?

d
No, gracias, ¿cuánto es todo?
Adiós.
Y 5€ de cambio, ¡gracias!
Son 25€.
De nada, adiós.
Muy bien, ¿algo más?
Aquí tiene.

C Now listen and check you got the dialogue in the right order.

D Cover the pictures above. Listen again and say if the following statements are true or false.

1 El vino de Rioja está de oferta.

2 El cliente compra tres botellas de vino.

3 El vino de Valdepeñas es barato y bueno.

4 El precio del vino de Ribeiro es 15€.

5 En la tienda venden cinco tipos de vinos españoles.

2 En el bar

A Read and listen to the dialogue, then decide if the following statements are true or false.

Camarero:	¿Qué van a tomar?
Cliente:	Para mí, un tinto reserva y una caña para mi amigo.
Camarero:	Muy bien, ahora mismo.
Cliente:	¿Tiene tapas?
Camarero:	Sí, hay tapas de tortilla, chorizo …

1 The customer is on his own in the bar.

2 The customer asks for some wine.

3 The waiter says he will get the drinks straight away.

4 The waiter says he hasn't got any tapas.

LEARNING TIP:

tomar el vermú

Tomar el vermú is a very Spanish custom, especially at weekends. The expression does not necessarily mean *to drink vermouth*, but *to have an aperitif*. It can be beer, wine, vermouth, anything you have before lunch.

¿Qué va(n) a tomar?

The waiter uses the expression **¿Qué van a tomar?** because he is talking to more than one person. When addressing one person, he would say **¿Qué va a tomar?** In both cases, this means *What would you like?*

para

Para mí means *for me*.

caña

Una caña is the equivalent of a half of lager.

¿tiene? / ¿hay?

Instead of **tiene**, you can also say **hay** meaning *Is there..?*: ¿Hay tapas?

CARTA DE VINOS

Reserva = Rva   Crianza = Cr

| El tinto de la casa | Corcovo Cr'97 | Valdepeñas. Sensible | 9,02€ |
| El blanco de la casa | Martivilli 2000 | Rueda. Verdejo | 7,21€ |

LISTA DE VINOS TINTOS

Gran Feudo	Rva'96	Navarra. Tempranillo	10,82€
Bach	Cr'96	Penedes. Merlot	9,02€
La Vicalanda	Rva'96	La Rioja. Tempranillo	15, 03€
Carchelo	2000	Jumilla. Tempranillo	9,02€
Campillo	Rva'92	La Rioja. Tempranillo	29,45 € 'Magnum'
Pago de Carraovejas	Cr'98	Rivera del Duero. Tinto país	15,03€
Viña Selentina	2000	Chile Cabernet Sauvignon	14,00€

LISTA DE VINOS BLANCOS

Marin Codas	2000	Rias Baixas Albariño	10,82€
Viña Esmeralda	2000	Penedés Moscatel/Gewurztraminer	7,81€
Viñas del Vero	1998	Sotontano Chardonnay	10,82€
Beringer Napa Valley	2000	California Chardonnay	29€

LISTA DE VINOS ROSADOS

| Torres de Casta | 2000 | Caiñena. Garnacha | 6,01€ |
| Cinco Almudes | 2000 | La Mancha. Garnacha | 5.41€ |

Mesón 'El Cojo'

Tapas y Raciones

aceitunas variadas 2€	berenjenas de Almagro 3€
almendras saladas 1,50€	calabacines rellenos 3€
patatas a lo pobre 4,50€	champiñones al ajillo 3,50€
patatas al alioli 4,50€	revuelto de setas 3,50€
patatas bravas 4,50€	tabla de embutidos 12€
tortilla de patatas 5€	jamón serrano 10€
pulpo a la gallega 7,50€	pata negra 15€
mejillones a la vinagreta 6€	lomo ibérico 12€
boquerones en vinagre 5€	chorizo al vino 6€
gambas a la plancha 8€	pollo al ajillo 5,50€
gambas al ajillo 8€	carne adobada 6,50€
gambas rebozadas 8€	pincho moruno 2,50€
calamares a la romana 6,50€	albóndigas con tomate 5€
sepia a la plancha 7,50€	morcilla de Burgos 5€
sardinas a la plancha 5€	croquetas de jamón 4,50€
pimientos asados 5,50€	croquetas de pescado 4,50€
asadillo 5,50€	tabla de quesos 8€
pisto manchego 5€	queso manchego 6€
	queso de cabrales 7€
	queso gallego 5€

B Can you work out what is on the board? You can probably guess some words.

1 How many meat tapas can you find?

2 And fish tapas?

3 Are there any vegetarian tapas?

Check with a partner.

C Listen to this group of friends in the 'Mesón El Cojo' and note down the tapas they order.

D Listen again. Did they order drinks, and if they did, what did you order?

LEARNING TIP:
Drinks

Un refresco is a soft drink like cola, lemonade, etc.:

un refresco de naranja, un refresco de limón

Un batido is a milkshake:

un batido de chocolate, un batido de fresa, un batido de plátano

Tapas

A **tapa** is a small portion of food which you receive when you buy a drink. Giving customers **tapas** is a custom throughout Spain. In some places, the **tapas** are free. They can vary from just a few nuts or a small dish of olives to almost a mini-meal in itself. If the portion is bigger, it is called a **ración** and you have to pay for it.

One of the greatest pleasures of being in Spain is to go out with your friends for **tapas (ir de tapas)**. It is a very sensible way of drinking because you eat as you drink. It is normal to stay in each tapas bar for only one or two drinks, so you may visit a whole series of bars during an evening.

If you look in the dictionary, you'll see that the word **tapa** literally means *lid* or *cover*. Some people will tell you that the word **tapa** for food originated because the glasses were physically covered by a small plate of or piece of food. Another explanation is that **tapas** 'cover' the appetite.

El restaurante

UNIT **5**

E  Imagine you are with a group of friends in the 'Mesón El Cojo'; you are the only Spanish speaker. Which dishes would you suggest to the following friends?

1 Charlie is a strict vegetarian.

2 Karen is a meat eater.

3 Simon loves seafood.

4 Robert likes spicy food.

5 Sarah can't eat eggs or dairy products.

F Write a conversation between you and a waiter in which you are ordering a drink and a tapa of your choice. Remember that to call the attention of the waiter or any other person, you can say **Oiga**, **por favor**, which means *Excuse me, please*.

There is further practice in ordering food and drink in Spanish on our website.

READY TO MOVE ON?

Check that you can...

- read and understand a *Ración* or *Tapas* menu
- order a drink and a snack in a bar
- pay for your order

3 Cenar o comer fuera

A  The 'Mesón El Cojo' also has a very good restaurant. Here are the dishes that they serve. You can probably guess some words from the context. Can you write them in the correct place on the menu? Listen and check.

Flan de la casa 4,50€
Flan de huevo con nata y fresas

Ternera empanada 12,95€
Filete de ternera rebozado en huevo pan y frito con patatas fritas y ensalada

Besugo al horno 12,95€
Besugo asado a fuego muy lento con patatas asadas y verduras del día

Ensalada mixta 5€
Ensalada de tomate, pepino, lechuga, huevo y aceitunas

Cochinillo 15,50€
Cerdo muy tierno asado con verduras

Plato de la casa 10,76€
Alcachofas, berenjenas, calabacines, pimientos asados y marinados en aceite de oliva servidos con una selección de embutidos

Sopa del día 5,45€
Sopa casera del día

Tabla de quesos 6,95€
Selección de quesos con uvas

Merluza a la romana 15,04€
Filete de merluza rebozada en harina, huevo y frita. Servida con patatas fritas y guisantes

Especialidad del chef 7,23€
Tostada de pan con aceite de oliva, ajo, tomate y jamón serrano

Lenguado a la plancha 11,89€
Lenguado pasado ligeramente por la plancha. Servido con ensalada y patatas fritas

Especialidad de la casa 15,50€
Pez espada adobado con ensalada mixta

Pescaditos fritos 11,50€
Combinado de pescados de la temporada

Chuletas de cordero lechal 16,34€
Chuletas de cordero a la plancha con puré de patata y ensalada mixta

Pechuga de pollo gratinada 12€
Pechuga de pollo rellena de ajo, champiñones y queso

Macedonia de frutas 5,25€
Elaborada con fruta del tiempo

Helados variados 5,57€
Copa con tres bolas de helado: nata, chocolate y fresa

Menu A La Carta

Primer plato

~

Segundo plato
Carnes

~

Pescados

~

Postre

UNIT **5**

B Can you work out the following common terms on the menu? Write a phrase using each one.

Example: del tiempo = *of the season*, e.g. fruta del tiempo

1 de la casa / casera   **2** del día   **3** mixta   **4** varios

C Look at the menu in activity 3A and imagine that you are the waiter. Explain the following terms to the customers. Answer their questions in English.

Examples: ¿Qué es la macedonia de frutas? → *It's a fruit salad made with fruit of the season.*

¿Qué lleva la ensalada mixta? → *It has tomato, cucumber, egg and olives.*

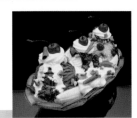   

1 ¿Qué lleva el helado variado?   **3** ¿Qué es la sopa casera?

2 ¿Qué es la ternera empanada?   **4** ¿Qué lleva la tabla de quesos?

D Listen to the dialogue and take a note of the order. Then add up the bill (**la cuenta**). Look at the wine list on page 72 and the menu on page 75 if you need help.

Restaurante El Cojo

Mesa n°	
Primer plato	
Segundo plato	
Postre y Cafés	
Bebidas	
Propina	Total

E A C (►) Look again at the menu in activity 3A and the bill you completed in activity 3D. What differences can you find between the bill and the dialogue below?

Camarero: Buenas noches.

Tú: Buenas noches, una mesa para dos.

Camarero: ¿Tiene reservada mesa?

Tú: No, lo siento.

Camarero: Un momento … Tenemos esa mesa libre.

Tú: Estupendo, muchas gracias.

Camarero: Aquí tienen el menú.

Tú: ¿Cuál es el vino de la casa?

Camarero: Es un vino de Rioja.

Tú ¿Qué lleva el plato de la casa?

Camarero El plato de la casa lleva pescados variados con ensalada.

Tú: Pues, de primero el plato de la casa para dos y para beber una botella de tinto de la casa.

Camarero: Muy bien, el plato de la casa y ¿de segundo?

Tú: Pez espada con ensalada para mi amiga y las chuletas de cordero para mí.

Camarero: ¿Cómo las quiere? ¿Muy hechas, hechas o poco hechas?

Tú: Las quiero poco hechas.

***

Camarero: Las chuletas de cordero.

Tú: Para mí.

Camarero: Y el pez espada para la señora.

Tú: Sí.

Camarero: Buen, provecho.

***

Camarero: ¿Quieren postre?

Tú: No, gracias.

Camarero: ¿Cafés?

Tú: Sí, uno solo y un cortado.

LEARNING TIP:
Phrases

Una mesa para … *A table for …*

¿Tiene reservada mesa?
Have you booked a table?

Tengo reservada mesa.
I have booked a table.

libre   *free, available*

Hot drinks

- There are various ways in which coffee is served:

  Espresso: usually served black (**café solo**)

  Café cortado: an espresso with a dash of milk

  Café con leche: half coffee, half warm milk

  Café americano: a large, weak coffee

  Carajillo: coffee with brandy

  Café con hielo: black coffee served cold over ice cubes

- Herbal tea is very popular. The most common varieties are: **manzanilla** (camomile), **poleo menta** (mint tea), **mate** (very popular in Argentina, Paraguay, Uruguay and southern Brazil).

- **Chocolate** (thick, sweet hot chocolate) is a very popular early-morning drink. **Chocolate con churros** (hot chocolate with a type of doughnut) is a typical Spanish breakfast, and also a mid-afternoon snack: **La merienda**.

5

You'll find more practice using *gustar* c
www.accesslanguages.co

✓

Check that you ...
- understand and ask about items on a menu
- can order a meal from a menu

4 Me gusta la paella

LANGUAGE FOCUS

gustar

To express likes and dislikes, you use the verb **gustar**.

Gustar literally means 'to please', and the thing that is liked is the subject of the verb. So if that thing is singular, you use **gusta**; if it is plural, you use **gustan**. The pronoun before the verb indicates the person who does the liking.

me gusta / me gustan	*I like*
te gusta / te gustan	*you like* (informal singular)
le gusta / le gustan	*he/she likes / you like* (formal singular)
nos gusta / nos gustan	*we like*
os gusta / os gustan	*you like* (informal plural)
les gusta / les gustan	*they like / you like* (formal plural)

Me gusta la paella.	*I like paella.*
Nos gusta el vino.	*We like wine.*

Me gustan los mariscos.	*I like seafood.*
Les gustan las espinacas.	*They like spinach.*

Gustar is also used in the singular followed by a verb:

Me gusta beber vinos españoles.	*I like drinking Spanish wines.*
Le gusta comer paella.	*He likes eating paella.*

To express dislikes, just put **no** in front:

No me gusta el café.	*I don't like coffee.*
No les gusta comer galletas.	*They don't like eatimg biscuits.*

Me gusta(n) muchísimo ...	*I like ... very much.* ☺☺☺
Me gusta(n) mucho ...	*I like ... a lot.* ☺☺
Me gusta(n) ...	*I like ...* ☺
No me gusta(n) ...	*I don't like ...* ☹
No me gusta(n) nada ...	*I don't like ... at all.* ☹☹

Use the ending **-ísimo/a** to say you like something very much. This ending can also be added to adjectives to say when something is extremely good or extremely bad.

El queso está buenísimo; Los quesos españoles están buenísimos.
La fruta está buenísima; Las frutas del bosque están buenísimas.

A ✍ ▷ Complete this dialogue between two friends with the correct form of **gustar**. Remember to look at who is doing the action.

(A) ¿Qué ⬭ ⬭ comer?

(B) ⬭ ⬭ las verduras.

(A) ¿ ⬭ ⬭ la col (*cabbage*)?

(B) Sí, pero a mi marido no ⬭ ⬭ la col. A él no ⬭ ⬭ las verduras, sólo ⬭ ⬭ la carne y el pescado. Y a ti, ¿qué ⬭ ⬭ ?

(A) ⬭ ⬭ los helados.

B 🎧 ▷ Listen and check.

C ✍ ▷ Your friend has invited you for lunch and you want to compliment him/her on the food. What would you say about these dishes?

Ejemplo: spinach → Las espinacas me gustan mucho.

1 mushrooms **2** beans **3** meat **4** wine

D 🎧 ▷ Listen to a couple talking to the waiter at the 'Mesón El Cojo' about their dinner. What did they think of it?

5 ¿Le apetece un licor?

A 🔊 ▷ What would you say if you wanted to invite your friend to …

1 have another drink ?

2 dance (**bailar**)?

3 go out for lunch?

4 go for a drink?

5 see a movie (**ver una película**)?

6 go shopping?

B 🔊 ▷ Answer the invitations by accepting three and refusing two.

> **LEARNING TIP:**
> There are different ways to invite someone to do something.
> To a friend say:
> ¿**Quieres** una cerveza?
> ¿**Quieres** cenar conmigo?
> ¿**Te apetece** tomar algo?
> To a person you do not know, use the polite form:
> ¿**Quiere** una cerveza?
> ¿**Quiere** cenar conmigo?
> ¿**Le apetece** tomar algo?
> To accept, say:
> Vale.
> Muy bien.
> Gracias.
> To refuse, say:
> No, gracias.
> Lo siento, no puedo. (*I'm sorry, I can't.*)

C The waiter has come back with more coffee. Read and listen to the dialogue and answer the questions.

Camarero: ¿Les apetece un licor de manzana, de melón …? Invita la casa.
Tú: Vale, muchas gracias.

Tú: Camarero, la cuenta, por favor.
Camarero: Un momento.

Camarero: Aquí tienen.
Tú: ¿Está la propina incluida?
Camarero: No.
Tú: Aquí tiene, quédese con el cambio.
Camarero: Muchas gracias.
Tú: De nada.
Camarero: Adiós.
Tú: Adiós.

1 What does the waiter offer them to drink?
2 Do they have to pay for the drinks?

hispanic world

One of the most common drinks in the Latino world is the **cubalibre** (rum and cola). Rum (**el ron**) is produced in most Central American and Caribbean counties, such as Cuba. There is a large variety of cocktails made with rum. Two of them, Mojito and Daiquiri, were made famous by Hemingway.

If you would like more information about recipes for cocktails, check out our website.

Cavas

Castell Blanch.	Extra.	Cava. Macabeo, Parellada y xarel-lo	6,01 €
Juve y Camps	Rva. Familia	Cava. Macabeo, Parellada y xarel-lo	22,30 €

Lista de vinos de postre

Solera 1847	Oloroso dulce. Jerez	1,20 € copa
Fusta Nova2000	Valencia. Moscatel	7,21 € 50cl
Gran Barquero	Motilla Moriles. Pedro Ximenez	1,80 € copa

Brandys, licores y digestivos

Torres 10	3€ copa
Lepanto Solera Gran Reseva	7,85€ copa
Gran Duque de Alba Solera Gran Reserva 1866	9,99€ copa
Aguaardiente Adega Velha da casa D'Avellada.	
Reserva. Edición numerada y limitada	10,85€
Cuervo especial	5€ copa
Chivas Regal 12 años	9,10€ copa
Jack Daniels Tennessee	7,20€ copa
Habana Club 7 años añejo	9€ copa
Varadero Cubano 7 años	6,90€ copa

READY TO MOVE ON?

✓

Check that you can...
- say what you like and don't like
- pay compliments
- accept and decline invitations

El restaurante UNIT 5

Descubre el mundo HISPANO

La comida Tex Mex

El estilo de comida llamado "Tex Mex" combina elementos (ingredientes, métodos de preparación) mexicanos y estadounidenses. Frecuentemente ocupa "alimentos de conveniencia" (congelados, enlatados) — comúnes en los Estados Unidos — para hacer más fácil y rápida la preparación. Aunque Tex Mex tiene algo en común con las cocinas mexicana y americana, no se le puede considerar ni comida auténticamente mexicana ni típicamente estadounidense.

Una receta de cocina: Sopa de chili tex-mex

- un kilo de carne de ternera picada, pasada por la sartén y escurrida
- dos latas de tomates enteros (de 400 gramos cada una)
- 400 gramos de champiñones en rodajas
- dos latas de salsa de tomate (de 400 gramos cada una)
- una lata de pasta de tomate (de 400 gramos)
- dos latas de frijoles (colorados), escurridas (de 400 gramos cada una)
- una cebolla grande trozeada
- dos pimientos jalapeños, sin semillas y cortados a rodajas finas
- un diente de ajo machacado
- tres cucharadas de chili en polvo
- una cucharada de comino

Mezclar todos los ingredientes y cocinar. Para conseguir un sabor y una textura ideal, cocinar en el microondas a una temperatura media durante treinta o cuarenta minutos. De vez en cuando, remover la mezcla. Si lo prefiere, el chili se puede cocinar usando el método tradicional en una olla en la cocina. ¡Riquísimo!

A Answer the questions about the text above and the recipe.

1 What does Tex Mex food combine?

2 What kind of ingredients are used in the US to make Tex Mex cooking easier?

3 Which are the main ingredients of the chili soup?

4 Is the recipe very complicated?

B Write a brief summary (about five lines) explaining what type of cuisine you like and why.

GLOSSARY

Nouns

aceitunas (fpl)	olives
ajo (m)	garlic
alcachofa (f)	artichoke
almendras (fpl)	almonds
asadillo (m)	roasted peppers
berenjena (f)	aubergine
besugo (m)	sea bream
bola (f)	scoop
calabacín (m)	courgette
cambio (m)	change
chile (m)	chilli
chocolate (m)	(hot) chocolate
chuleta (f)	chop
cochinillo (m)	roast suckling pig
col (f)	cabbage
copa (f)	(wine) glass
cortado (m)	coffee with a dash of milk
croqueta (f)	croquette
cuenta (f)	bill
empanada (f)	meat or fish pie
ensalada (f)	salad
espinacas (fpl)	spinach
filete (m)	fillet
flan (m)	crème caramel
fresa (f)	strawberry
harina (f)	flour
helado (m)	ice cream
lenguado (m)	sole
licor (m)	liqueur
macedonia (f)	fruit salad

mariscos (mpl)	seafood
menú (m)	menu
nata (f)	cream
paella (valenciana) (f)	paella
pechuga de pollo (f)	chicken breast
pez espada (m)	swordfish
postre (m)	dessert
primer plato (m)	first course
propina (f)	tip
pulpo (m)	octopus
ración (f)	portion
revuelto (m)	scrambled eggs
segundo plato (m)	second/main course
setas (fpl)	wild mushrooms
sopa (f)	soup
tortilla (de patatas) (f)	(potato) omelette
vermut (m)	vermouth
vinagre (m)	vinegar
zumo (m)	juice

Adjectives

adobado/a	seasoned, prepared
asado/a	roast(ed)
casero/a	homemade, of the house
crudo/a	raw
empanada	fried in breadcrumbs
frito/a	fried
gratinado/a	with grated cheese
hecho/a	done, prepared
ibérico/a	Iberian

El restaurante

UNIT **5**

GLOSSARY

libre	free, available
mixto/a	mixed
rebozado/a	rolled in (breadcrumbs)
relleno/a	stuffed
reservada/o	booked
salado/a	salted
típico/a	typical
variado/a	varied, different

Verbs

apetecer	to appeal to, fancy
cenar	to have dinner
cenar fuera	to go out for dinner
comer	to eat, have lunch
comer fuera	to go out for lunch
encantar	to love, like very much
gustar	to like
llevar	to contain
poder	to be able to
tomar	to take, eat, drink

Expressions

a la plancha	grilled
a la romana	battered
al horno	in the oven
Buen provecho.	Enjoy your meal.
de cabrales	goat's
de la casa	house
del día	of the day
del tiempo	of the season
empanada	fried in breadcrumbs
ir de tapas	to go for tapas
Lo siento.	I'm sorry.
¡Oiga!	Excuse me!
Para mí.	For me.
una tabla de quesos	a cheeseboard

 # LOOKING FORWARD

In the next unit, we will look at giving directions and finding places. We will also have a brief look at the weather.

To prepare, make a list of local amenities and types of shops to be found in a town or a city (use a dictionary if necessary).

Look at the map and try to understand the sentences.

Canadá está en el norte de América.

Chile está en el sur de América.

Uruguay está al este de Argentina.

Perú está al oeste de Brasil.

Panamá está en el centro de América.

Paraguay está lejos de Estados Unidos.

Honduras está cerca de Nicaragua.

Puerto Rico está enfrente de República Dominicana.

Ecuador está entre Colombia y Perú.

Guatemala está al lado del Salvador...

El restaurante

UNIT 6
¿Dónde está?

> **By the end of this unit you will be able to:**
>
> - Say what there is in your town/city
> - Ask for and understand directions.
> - Give directions
> - Get around the town/city
> - Talk about the weather
> - Make comparisons

1 ¿Qué recuerdas?

A A C  Clasifica en categorías. Classify in groups.

- patatas bravas • calamares a la romana • vino tinto
- tortilla de patatas • cerveza • chorizo al vino
- champiñones rellenos • gambas al ajillo • pulpo a la gallega
- cava • sardinas a la plancha

Bebidas	Carnes	Pescados	Mariscos	Verduras

B  ¿Quién dice qué? ¿Camarero o cliente?
Who says what? The waiter or the customer?

1	Para mí …	**6**	Son treinta y cinco euros.
2	¿Qué van a tomar?	**7**	¿Qué lleva la tortilla española?
3	La cuenta, por favor.	**8**	Una mesa para cuatro.
4	¿Cuál es el vino de la casa?	**9**	Buen provecho.
5	¿Va a tomar café?	**10**	¿Tiene reservada mesa?

2 ¿Qué hay en tu pueblo?

A Marco está en la oficina de turismo de Barcelona, quiere saber qué lugares interesantes hay para visitar. Escucha y marca los lugares que oigas.

Marco is in the tourist information office in Barcelona. He wants to know what places there are. Listen and tick the places you hear.

bares	
palacios	
catedrales	
restaurantes	
teatros	
piscinas	
tiendas	
galerías de arte	
ayuntamiento	
comisaría	
museos	
playa	

¿Dónde está? UNIT **6**

LANGUAGE FOCUS

hay

You already know the expression **hay** to ask about availability.

¿**Hay** tapas?   –Sí, **hay** tapas de aceitunas, tortilla, champiñones …

Hay is also used to talk about facilities:
En Barcelona hay muchos teatros.

In both cases, **hay** can be used in a similar way to **tener**:

¿**Tiene** tapas?   –Sí, **tenemos** tapas de aceitunas, tortilla, champiñones …

Barcelona **tiene** muchos teatros.

Talking about where things are

¿Qué hay en …?	*What is there in …?*
Hay …	*There is/are …*
¿Hay …?	*Is/Are there … ?*
por aquí	*near here*
cerca/lejos	*near/far*

Perdone, ¿hay un parque por aquí?
Excuse me, is there a park near here?

Sí, hay uno/a.	*Yes, there's one*
dos, tres, cuatro …	*two, three, four …*
algunos/as; varios/as	*some; several*
muchos/as	*many*
No, no hay.	*No, there isn't/aren't.*

B Mira el plano del centro de Madrid y haz una lista de lo que hay y cuantos/as. No olvides mencionar algo que no hay (utiliza las expresiones mencionadas arriba).

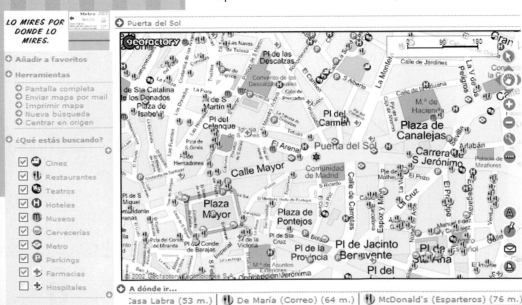

Look at the map of Madrid city centre and make a list of what places there are and how many, e.g. Hay varios hoteles y muchos restaurantes.
Don't forget to mention something that isn't there. Use the expressions listed above.

C Escucha a Eva hablar sobre el centro de Madrid y comprueba tu respuesta. ¿Qué diferencias hay entre su respuesta y la tuya?
Listen to Eva talking about Madrid city centre and compare her comments with yours. Are there any differences?

D Habla de los lugares en tu pueblo/ciudad con tu compañero/a.
Practise talking about places in town with a partner.

A ¿Hay una farmacia por aquí?

B Sí, hay una en la Puerta del Sol.

A ¿Está cerca?

B No, está lejos, muy lejos.

3 ¿Dónde está la Puerta del Sol?

A Lee el texto y mira los diagramas. ¿Qué mapa representa la ruta?
Read the text and look at the diagrams. Which map shows the correct route?

Está lejos, a unos 500 metros, siga todo recto y tome la primera calle a la derecha y la segunda calle a la izquierda: está al final de la calle.

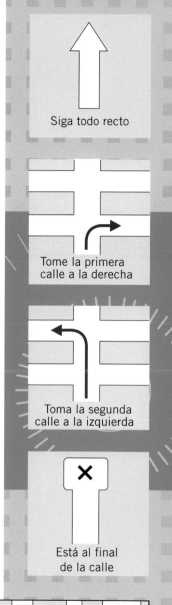

Siga todo recto

Tome la primera
calle a la derecha

Toma la segunda
calle a la izquierda

Está al final
de la calle

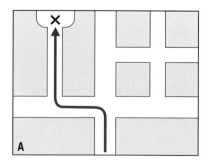

A

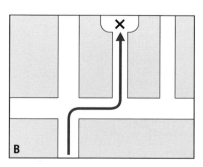

B

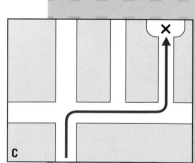

C

¿Dónde está? UNIT 6

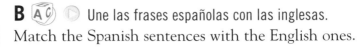

B Une las frases españolas con las inglesas.
Match the Spanish sentences with the English ones.

Block is **manzana** in
Spain, but **cuadra** in
Latin America.

Practise saying where places are on
www.accesslanguages.com

1	Está en el centro.	**a**	It's in the south.
2	Está a veinticinco minutos andando / a pie.	**b**	It's three kilometres from here.
3	Está a tres kilómetros.	**c**	It's in the north.
4	Está en el norte.	**d**	It's in the west.
5	Está en el oeste.	**e**	It's 25 minutes' walk away.
6	Está en el este.	**f**	It's in the east.
7	Está en el sur.	**g**	It's in the centre.
8	Está a dos manzanas.	**h**	It's two blocks away.

C Ahora mira los mapas de Madrid (página 88) y sus alrededores más de cerca (abajo) y di dónde están los siguientes lugares. Tú estás en la Puerta del Sol. Now look at the maps of Madrid and the surrounding area. Say where the following places are. You are in La Puerta del Sol.

1 ¿Dónde está la Comunidad de Madrid?

2 ¿Dónde está la Carrera San Jerónimo?

3 ¿Dónde está Navacerrada?

4 ¿Dónde está la plaza de las Descalzas?

5 ¿Dónde está Chinchón?

6 ¿Dónde está la calle Tetuán?

7 ¿Dónde está Aranjuez?

8 ¿Dónde está Colmenar Viejo?

4 ¿Ser o no ser?

LANGUAGE FOCUS

In Unit 3, we saw that there are two verbs in Spanish which mean *to be*.

Ser is used to say: who you are, where you are from, what you look like (i.e. to describe yourself) and what you do for a living.

Ésta **es** Carmen. Carmen **es** mi amiga, **es** chilena. Ella es morena, alta, guapa y simpática. Carmen y yo **somos** estudiantes.

Estar is used to say: how you are, if you are single or married, and also to say where a place is:

¿Cómo **estás**?   **Estoy** bien, gracias.
¿**Estás** casada?   No, **estoy** soltera.
¿Dónde **está** Carmen?   **Está** en el museo.

A Di estas frases en español.
Can you say the following in Spanish?

1 I'm Sabrina, I'm a director.

2 How are you? –So-so.

3 Where is your boss?

4 Are you single? –Yes, I am.

5 Where are you from? –I am from Oscos.

6 Oscos, where is Oscos?

7 It's in Asturias, Spain.

8 Is this your boyfriend?

9 No, he is small, ugly and unfriendly.

10 My boyfriend is tall, blond, handsome, strong and very nice.

B Escucha y comprueba tus respuestas a la actividad 4A.

Practise using **ser** and **estar** on
www.accesslanguages.com

¿Dónde está? UNIT 6

5 ¿Dónde está(n)?

A ¿Cómo preguntarías por … ?
How would you ask for…?

1	the town hall	**4**	the shops
2	the bars	**5**	the cathedral
3	the police station	**6**	the square

LANGUAGE FOCUS

¿Dónde está el mecánico?

delante de

detrás de

al lado de

enfrente de

entre … y …

en

en la esquina

a la derecha

a la izquierda

encima

When **de** or **a** are followed by **el**, the words are contracted:

a + el = al   de + el = del

al lado **del** coche

debajo

B 🎲 🔵 Mira el mapa y di si las siguientes afirmaciones son correctas o incorrectas. Si son incorrectas, corrígelas.

Look at the map and say if the following statements are true or false. Correct the false ones.

1 La estación de tren está en la esquina, al lado de la estación de autobuses.

2 El hotel está al lado del bar.

3 La plaza está en el centro.

4 El parque municipal está delante del bar 'El Penalty'.

5 El bar 'El Penalty' está delante del parque municipal.

6 El colegio está a la derecha del ayuntamiento.

7 La comisaría está entre el colegio y el hotel.

8 El ayuntamiento está a la izquierda del colegio.

9 El colegio está cerca de la plaza.

10 La estacion de autobuses está en la plaza.

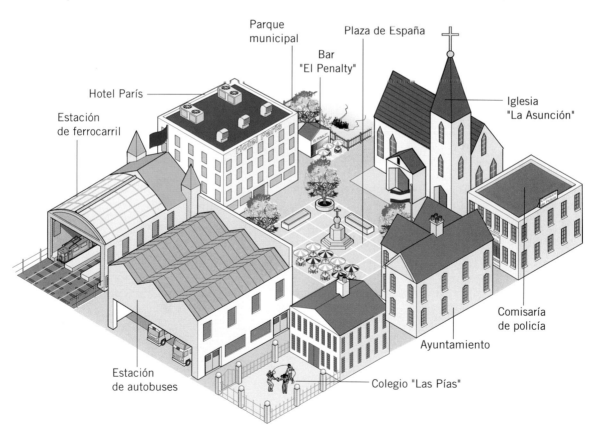

Parque municipal
Bar "El Penalty"
Plaza de España
Hotel París
Estación de ferrocarril
Iglesia "La Asunción"
Comisaría de policía
Ayuntamiento
Estación de autobuses
Colegio "Las Pías"

C 🔊 🔵 Escucha y corrige el mapa. Listen and correct the map.

¿Dónde está? UNI **6**

93

LANGUAGE FOCUS

Look at these commands. You use different forms, depending on whether you are addressing the person as **usted** or **tú**.

	Formal *(usted)*	Informal *(tú)*
take	tome	toma
follow	siga	sigue
turn	tuerza / doble	tuerce / dobla
cross	cruce	cruza

LEARNING TIP:
coger/tomar

In Spain, you will commonly hear **coge** or **coja** to mean *take* or *catch*. However, it is considered very impolite in Latin America, where **toma/tome** are used instead.

primero, segundo

The words for *first* (**primero**) and *second* (**segundo**) act like other adjectives and agree with the noun. However, sometimes the noun is omitted:

Para mí de **primero** [plato], sopa. Y de **segundo** [plato], carne.

La **primera** [calle] a la derecha y la **segunda** [calle] a la izquierda.

D 🎲 ▷ Une el vocabulario con los símbolos (usa el diccionario si lo necesitas).

Match the expressions with the symbols (use a dictionary if necessary).

1 todo recto / todo derecho   a   **2**

2 a la izquierda   b   ↑ (with line above)

3 a la derecha   c   ↑

4 primera   d   ↱

5 segunda   e   **3**

6 tercera   f   ↰

7 al final   g   **1**

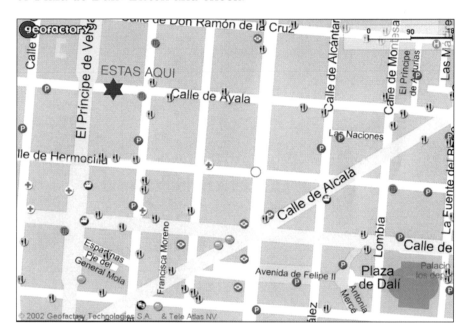

E [AC] (((·))) ▶ Mira el plano y lee las instrucciones ¿Cuál te lleva a la
Plaza de Dalí?

Look at the map and read the instructions. Which ones take you
to Plaza de Dalí? Listen and check.

Perdone, ¿dónde está la plaza de Dalí?

1 Siga todo recto y tome la cuarta a la derecha, continúe recto y cruce la
Calle de Alcalá, luego tome la primera a la izquierda, la Plaza de Dalí
está allí, en la esquina.

2 Está muy cerca; tome la primera a la derecha y luego la primera a la
izquierda, continúe recto, cruce la Calle de Alcalá y alli está.

3 Tome la primera a la izquierda y la primera a la derecha, siga todo recto
hasta el final, allí está, enfrente.

4 Está lejos, a unos quince minutos andando; todo recto y tome la tercera a
la derecha, continúe recto y tome la tercera a la izquierda, está allí, al
final de la calle a unos doscientos metros.

¿Dónde está? UNIT 6

F Vas a organizar una fiesta. En las invitaciones introduces una nota dando direcciones para que tus amigos encuentren tu piso. Mira el mapa y escribe las instrucciones, para ello sigue el camino marcado por las estrellas.

You are going to organize a party. You include a note with the invitations so your friends can find their way to your flat. Look at the map and write the directions, following the route marked by the stars.

FIESTA EN MI CASA

MAÑANA A LAS 20:00

TE ESPERO EN

Calle Esparteros, 12

G Escucha a Eva dándo instrucciones de cómo llegar a su casa desde la estación de metro. (Fíjate: usa la forma familiar.) Sólo una de ellas es correcta, ¿cuál es? Completa el cuadro.

Listen to Eva giving directions from the underground station to her house. (Note that she uses the **tú** form.) Only one set of directions is correct. Which one? Complete the grid.

	Correcta	Incorrecta	Te lleva a … *(It takes you to …)*
1			
2			
3			

For more practice on giving directions, consult our website.

LEARNING TIP:

Here are some key words which will help in many situations:

Lo siento.	*I'm sorry.*
No entiendo.	*I don't understand.*
No sé.	*I don't know.*
¿Puede repetir?	*Could you repeat that?*
¿Puede hablar más despacio?	*Could you speak more slowly?*
Pues, …	*Well, …*

READY TO MOVE ON?

✓

Check that you can …

- ask and say what there is in a town and how many amenities there are
- understand distances
- talk about where places are in relation to each other
- understand more about the differences between *ser* and *estar*
- ask for and give directions

6

6 ¿Qué tiempo hace?

LANGUAGE FOCUS

In Unit 2, the verb **hacer** was used to ask what someone does for a living. It is also used when talking about the weather.

Hace buen tiempo.	*The weather is nice.*
Hace mal tiempo.	*The weather is bad.*
Hace calor.	*It is hot.*
Hace frío.	*It is cold.*
Hace sol.	*It is sunny.*
Hace viento.	*It is windy.*
Hace fresco.	*It is chilly.*

Note: since Spanish uses nouns in weather expressions – **el calor**, **el frío**, **el sol**, etc. –

instead of adjectives, as in English, the idea of *very/a lot* is expressed by **mucho** (not **muy**).

Hace **mucho calor**.   *It's very hot.*
Hace **mucho viento**.   *It's very windy.*

There are some weather expressions that don't use **hacer**:

Está nublado.	*It is cloudy.*
Llueve.	*It is raining / It rains.*
Nieva.	*It is snowing / It snows.*

En Inglaterra **llueve** mucho y en los Andes **nieva** mucho.
In England it rains a lot and in the Andes it snows a lot.

LEARNING TIP:

la nube = *cloud*
la lluvia = *rain*
la nieve = *snow*

A Mira las fotos y explica el tiempo que hace.
Look at the pictures and say what the weather's like.

Ejemplo: ¿Qué tiempo hace hoy?
Hoy hace viento, mucho frío y llueve.

1 ¿Qué tiempo hace en primavera?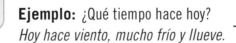

2 ¿Qué tiempo hace en verano?

3 ¿Qué tiempo hace en otoño?

4 ¿Qué tiempo hace en invierno?

B Explica cómo es el tiempo en tu región durante las cuatro estaciones.

Describe what the weather is like in your region in each season.

C Escucha el pronóstico de hoy y di de qué mapa está hablando.

Listen to today's weather forecast and say which map it is describing.

7 Hace más calor que en España

map 1

map 2

LANGUAGE FOCUS

Comparaciones

There are three main ways of comparing things in Spanish:

1 Equality (*as … as …*)

If the comparison is based on an adjective, the expression to use is:

tan + adjective + **como**

Alaska es **tan** fría **como** la Tierra del Fuego.

Alaska is as cold as Tierra del Fuego.

If the comparison is based on a noun, use:

tanto/a/os/as + noun + **como**

En Buenos Aires hay **tantos** teatros **como** en Nueva York.

In Buenos Aires, there are as many theatres as in New York.

2 Superiority (*bigger/more … than*) Use:

más + adjective/noun + **que**

Perú es **más** grande **que** Ecuador.

Peru is bigger than Ecuador.

Chile tiene **más** costa **que** Ecuador.

Chile has more coastline than Ecuador.

3 Inferiority (*smaller/less … than*) Use:

menos + adjective/noun + **que**

Ecuador es **menos** grande **que** Perú.

Ecuador is smaller than Peru.

Ecuador tiene **menos** costa **que** Chile.

Ecuador has less coastline than Chile.

A Forma frases comparativas. Write comparative sentences.

Ejemplos: Cuba / Argentina / calor → *En Cuba hace más calor que en Argentina.*

Costa Rica / EEUU / España / cerca → *Costa Rica está más cerca de EEUU que España.*

1 México / Chile / frío

2 Panamá / Honduras / Perú / lejos

3 Venezuela / Colombia / calor

4 Ecuador / Uruguay / sol

5 Andes peruanos / Andes bolivianos / fresco

6 Honduras / Guatemala / Paraguay / cerca

For more activities on this unit, go to our website www.accesslanguages.com

READY
TO MOVE ON?

Check that you can...

☐ ask and say what the weather is like

☐ make comparisons

CHILE

Superficie: 756.945 km²
Situación: sector occidental de Sudamérica
Largo: 4.200 km de norte a sur
Límites: Norte: Perú; Este: Bolivia y Argentina; Sur: Polo Sur;
Oeste: Océano Pacífico.
Población: 14.622.354 habitantes.
Idioma primario: Español
Otras lenguas: Mapuche, Quechua, Aymará y Pascuense
División administrativa: catorce regiones: Tarapacá,
Antofagasta, Atacama, Coquimbo, Valparaíso, Libertador
General Bernardo O'Higgins, Maule, Biobío, La Araucanía,
Los Lagos, Aisén del General Carlos Ibáñez del Campo,
Magallanes, Antártica y Metropolitana de Santiago;
51 provincias; 335 comunas.
Capital: Región Metropolitana de Santiago (Santiago de Chile)
Principales ciudades: Santiago, Valparaíso, Concepción,
Antofagasta y Temuco

 Clima

El extenso territorio chileno presenta diversos tipos de climas,
tales como desértico, estepárico mediterráneo, templado
cálido lluvioso, marítimo lluvioso, estepárico frío, de tundra y
polar. En la cordillera de los Andes impera el clima de altura
y en sus altas cumbres se da el clima de hielo.

Básicamente hablando, Chile posee un clima seco desde la primera hasta la cuarta región, donde las
lluvias son relativamente escasas. La sequía aumenta para el norte hacia las ciudades de Arica Iquique
y Antofagasta, ciudades que se caracterizan por sus escasas lluvias durante el año. La zona central de
Chile, que abarca la quinta región, región metropolitana, la sexta y séptima región, se caracteriza por
tener un clima más variado durante el año. En la temporada de invierno las temperaturas suelen ser
bajas y algunas veces llueve; en verano las temperaturas pueden alcanzar los 38 grados Celsius. En el
sur, que abarca desde la octava región hasta la duodécima región, las temperaturas durante el invierno
son muy bajas. Estas zonas se caracterizan por tener un alto índice de lluvias y bajas temperaturas en el
invierno, mientras más se avanza hacia el sur, el clima se hace más lluvioso y más helado. En verano, el
sur suele ser caluroso, pero no se escapa de las lluvias, la zona sur del país se caracteriza también por
tener lluvias durante el año.

A Escribe un resumen sobre la situación geográfica y clima de
Chile en un máximo de seis lineas.
Write a short summary describing Chile's geographical location
and climate in no more than six lines.

GLOSSARY

Nouns

alrededores (mpl)	surrounding area
ayuntamiento (m)	town hall
banco (m)	bank
biblioteca (f)	library
calle (f)	street
catedral (f)	cathedral
ciudad (f)	city
Correos (m)	post office
cuadra (f) (LA)	block
estación de tren/autobús (f)	train/bus station
este (m)	east
iglesia (f)	church
kilómetro (m)	kilometre
lluvia (f)	rain
manzana (f) (Sp)	block
metro (m)	underground station
nieve (f)	snow
norte (m)	north
oeste (m)	west
oficina de información (f)	tourist information office
otoño (m)	autumn
parque (m)	park
piscina (f)	swimming pool
plaza (f)	square
primavera (f)	spring
pueblo (m)	town, village
sur (m)	south
teatro (m)	theatre
tienda (f)	shop
verano (m)	summer

Adjectives

algunos/as	some
muchos/as	many
tercero/a	third
varios/as	various, several

Verbs

andar	to walk
coger	to catch, take
cruzar	to cross
doblar	to turn
llover	to rain
nevar	to snow
seguir	to follow
torcer	to turn

Prepositions

(a la) derecha	(on the) right
(a la) izquierda	(on the) left
al final	at the end
al lado de	next to, beside
cerca de	near
debajo de	under
delante de	in front of
detrás de	behind
en el centro	in the centre/middle

GLOSSARY

en la esquina	on the corner	Está nublado.	It's cloudy.
encima de	on top of	Hace buen tiempo.	The weather's nice.
enfrente de	opposite	Hace calor.	It's hot.
entre … y …	between … and …	Hace fresco.	It's chilly.
lejos (de)	far (from)	Hace frío.	It's cold.
		Hace mal tiempo.	The weather's bad.

Others

más que	more than	Hace sol.	It's sunny.
menos que	less than	Hace viento.	It's windy.
tan … como	as … as	¿Hay … ?	Is/Are there …?
tanto … como	as … as	por aquí	around/near here
		¿Tiene …?	Does it/he/she/you have …?

Expressions

a pie	on foot	todo recto	straight on
andando	walking, on foot		

LOOKING FORWARD

In **Unit 7**, we will be looking at the time and timetables.

Look at these train tickets and find out as much information as you can.

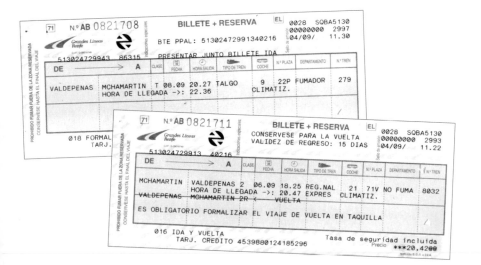

UNIT 7

Un billete, por favor

UNIT **6**

103

UNIT 7
Un billete, por favor

By the end of this unit you will be able to:

- Buy train/bus/plane tickets and check travel details
- Give the time and enquire about departure and arrival times
- Talk about days of the week, months of the year and dates
- Ask about and get around by public transport
- Ask about routes
- Use more comparatives and talk about your preferences
- Write informal letters
- Make requests using **puedo**

1 ¿Qué recuerdas?

A Pon las palabras en orden. Put the words in order.

Ejemplo: aquí supermercado un por hay ¿ ? → *¿Hay un supermercado por aquí?*

ACCESS SPANISH

1 principal dónde calle la está ¿ ?

2 calle la recto todo final de al

3 mercado esquina enfrente la está en del estanco el

4 muchísimo primavera calor hace en

5 llueve en no invierno

B  Escucha y contesta. Listen and answer these questions.

1 ¿Qué tiempo hace?

2 ¿Dónde es la barbacoa?

3 ¿Cómo se va a la barbacoa?

4 ¿Por qué hace la barbacoa?

C Escribe las instrucciones para llegar a estos lugares. Write instructions on how to get to the places below.

Estás en el ayuntamiento y quieres ir:

1 a la Giralda

2 al hospital Venerables

3 a la iglesia Santa Cruz

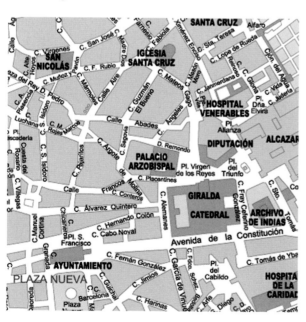

Un billete, por favor UNIT 7

2 Un billete

LANGUAGE FOCUS

The following table shows you how to ask for tickets.

Quisiera	un	boleto(s)							Fumador	
Quiero	dos	billete(s)	de ida →		para	Bilbao	en	primera 1ª	No fumador	
¿Tiene	tres		de ida y vuelta ↔			Madrid		segunda 2ª		
	cuatro					Barcelona				
	etc.									

A Pide los siguientes billetes. Ask for the following tickets.

Ejemplo: ↔ 1ª Ⓢ Sevilla x 1

Quiero un billete de ida y vuelta para Sevilla en primera, no fumador.

1. ↔ 2ª Ⓢ Gijón x 2
2. → 2ª Ⓢ Mérida x 1
3. ↔ 1ª Ⓢ Pamplona x 3
4. → 2ª Ⓢ Málaga x 1

B Escucha las conversaciones y numera los billetes en el orden en el que los oigas. Concentrate on the ticket type and number the tickets in the order you hear them.

a

```
CORDOBA
La Plata
CORDOBA
3456 589700
Segunda 26 V
23/09/
09:30
Ⓢ
```

b

```
ROSARIO
La Plata
ROSARIO
898775433598
Segunda 12P
18/03/
10:45
```

c

MENDOZA

38474887643
Primera 26 V
15/11/
13:00

d

SALTA
Tucumán
SALTA
876699654309
Primera 6 P
12/09/
22:50

e

TUCUMAN
Salta
TUCUMAN
28988753298
Segunda 65 P
31/08/
19:30

LEARNING TIP:

Notice that to say the date, you use **el** + day of the month + **de** + month

el 2 de diciembre

But if you want to include the day of the week, you don't use **el**:

lunes, 29 de abril

Capital letters are not used for months or days in Spanish.

3 El calendario y la hora

LANGUAGE FOCUS

Days and months

... y una semana tiene siete días.

El año tiene doce meses ...

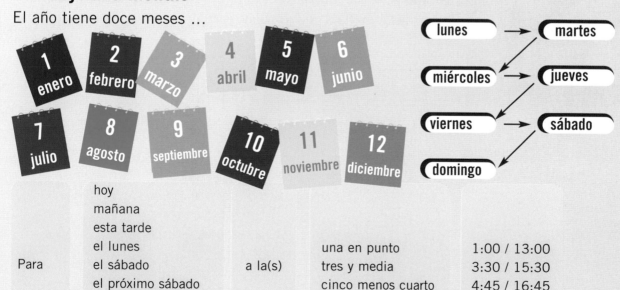

| 1 enero | 2 febrero | 3 marzo | 4 abril | 5 mayo | 6 junio |
| 7 julio | 8 agosto | 9 septiembre | 10 octubre | 11 noviembre | 12 diciembre |

lunes → martes
miércoles → jueves
viernes → sábado
domingo

| Para | hoy mañana esta tarde el lunes el sábado el próximo sábado el día 14 el 14 de septiembre | a la(s) | una en punto tres y media cinco menos cuarto | 1:00 / 13:00 3:30 / 15:30 4:45 / 16:45 |

A ¿Puedes aumentar la lista de posibles días y horas para viajar?
Can you add to the list with more days and times?

www.accesslanguages.com **has more practice in telling the time.**

B Escribe estas fechas, mira el calendario de este año y di en qué día de la semana caen.

Write these dates in full, then look at this year's calendar and say what day of the week they fall on.

Ejemplo: 28/07   *el veintiocho de julio   (miércoles), veintiocho de julio*
1 13/09   **2** 02/01   **3** 26/12   **4** 14/03

C Escucha de nuevo la actividad 2B y descubre si los días son los mismos en los billetes.

Listen to activity 2B again and see if the dates are the same as those on the tickets.

D Escucha y marca las horas que oigas. Listen and tick the times you hear on the bingo card.

E Ahora mira de nuevo el cartón de bingo y señala uno de los relojes que no han sido marcados. Luego pregunta a tu compañero/a la hora. Cambia papeles.

Now look at the bingo card again. Point to one of the clocks that hasn't been marked and ask your partner the time. Swap roles.

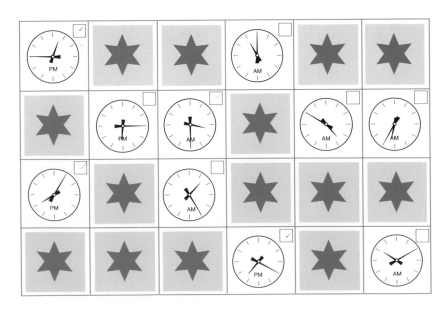

¿Qué hora es?

¿Qué hora es? What time is it?

- For times on the hour, use **Es/Son la(s) ....
  en punto.**

Es la una en punto.	1:00 / 13:00
Son las dos en punto.	2:00 / 14:00
Son las seis en punto.	6:00 / 18:00

- For half past the hour, use **Es/Son la(s) ...
  y media.**

Es la una y media.	1:30 / 13:30
Son las tres y media.	3:30 / 15:30
Son las siete y media.	7:30 / 19:30

- For quarter past the hour, use **Es/Son la(s) ...
  y cuarto.**

Es la una y cuarto.	1:15 / 13:15
Son las cuatro y cuarto.	4:15 / 16:15

- For other times past the hour, use **Es/Son la(s) ...
  y ...**

Es la una y veinte.	1:20 / 13:20
Son las cuatro y cinco.	4:05 / 16:05
Son las cinco y diez.	5:10 / 17:10

- For quarter to the hour, use **Es/Son la(s) ...
  menos ...**

Es la una menos cuarto.	12:45 / 00:45
Son las cuatro menos cuarto.	3:45 / 15:45

- For other times to the hour, use **Es/Son la(s) ...
  menos ...**

Es la una menos veinticinco.	12:35 / 00:35
Son las once menos veinte.	10:40 / 22:40

Es la ... is used for one o'clock (singular) only. All
other times use **Son las ...**

La(s) is used because the word **hora(s)** is understood,
but not stated.

LEARNING TIP:

The TALGO is a fast train, but
it's not the fastest; the AVE,
which runs between major cities,
is the fastest and travels up to
220mph.

último = *last*

7

LANGUAGE FOCUS

If you want to ask what time something happens, use **¿A qué hora ... ?**

¿A qué hora **sale** el autobús?   What time does the bus leave?

¿A qué hora **llega** el autobús?   What time does the bus arrive?

As in English, Spanish tends to use the twenty-four-hour clock for official timetables, such as trains and buses, or for offices hours.

F Mira el horario de trenes y contesta las preguntas. Look at the train timetable and answer the questions. Now listen to the recording and check your answers.

1   ¿A qué hora sale el TALGO de Mérida? 11.55

2   ¿A qué hora llega a Cáceres? 12.44

3   ¿A qué hora sale el primer tren de Mérida? 8.20

4   ¿A qué hora llega a Cáceres? 9.22

5   ¿A qué hora llega el último tren a Cáceres? 19.56

6   ¿A qué hora sale de Mérida? 18.59

Renfe - Horarios y Precios : Trenes entre CACERES y MERIDA

Estación Origen: Mérida   **Estación Destino:** Cáceres

Recorrido Tipo Tren	Salida	Llegada	Precios (euros)
Regional	08:20	09:22	3,25
TALGO	11:55	12:44	10,00
Regional	13:44	14:49	3,25
Regional	16:27	17:19	3,25
Triana	18:59	19:56	11,00

start   Renfe - Horarios y Pr...   Internet   19:05

G  Estudia el billete de tren y completa el diálogo como si tú fueras el cliente que compra el billete.

Study the train ticket and complete the dialogue as if you were the customer buying the ticket.

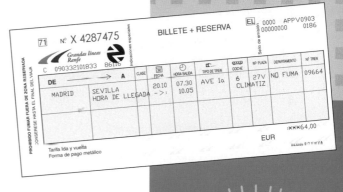

Empleado:	Buenos días.
Tú:	
Empleado:	¿Qué desea?
Tú:	
Empleado:	¿Lo quiere de ida o de ida y vuelta?
Tú:	
Empleado:	¿Para qué día?
Tú:	
Empleado:	¿Por la mañana o por la tarde?
Tú:	
Empleado:	Hay uno a las 7:30.
Tú:	
Empleado:	Llega a Sevilla a las 10:05. ¿Y la vuelta?
Tú:	
Empleado:	Hay uno a las 20:00.
Tú:	
Empleado:	Son 128 euros.
Tú:	
Empleado:	Su cambio.
Tú:	
Empleado:	De nada, adiós.

READY TO MOVE ON?

H Ahora escucha y comprueba tus respuestas. ¿Hay alguna diferencia?
Now listen and check your answers. Are there any differences?

Check that you can...

- understand and say the time and date
- ask and find out travel times and specify dates
- ask and understand the price
- buy a ticket and specify details

7

4 Quisiera más información

A (A C) ▷ Une las frases españolas con las inglesas.
Match the Spanish sentences with their English translations.

1	¿Es directo?	**a**	How can I get to … ?
2	¿Tengo que reservar plaza/asiento?	**b**	Do I have to get off at the next station?
3	¿Cómo puedo ir a … ?	**c**	Which platform does it leave from?
4	¿Puedo pagar en efectivo?	**d**	Can I pay cash?
5	¿Tengo que hacer transbordo?	**e**	Do I have to book a seat?
6	¿Tengo que bajar en la próxima estación?	**f**	Which platform does it arrive at?
7	¿De qué andén/vía sale?	**g**	Do I have to change?
8	¿A qué andén/vía llega?	**h**	Is it a through train?

B ◀))) ▷ Escucha los anuncios en el aeropuerto y corrige los errores.
Listen to the airport announcements and correct the mistakes.

Vuelo	Procedencia	Puerta	Llegada	Otra información
AV876	~~Bogotá~~ / *Caracas*	23	16:45	
AA674	La Paz	~~17~~ 16	17:26	Aterrizando
IB345	Madrid	15	17:35	~~10~~ 15 minutos de retraso

Vuelo	Destino	Puerta	Salida	Otra información
CO367	Quito	~~16~~ 17	16:15	
AR215	Asunción *Buenos Aires*	45	16:47	Vuelo directo
AA989	Los Angeles	2	17:25	Retraso *CANCELLED*

Puertas/*Gates*

Transbordo

C   Completa el diálogo. Complete the dialogue.

> barato   puedo   puede   rápido   más

Cliente: ¿Cómo (＿＿＿＿＿＿＿) ir al aeropuerto?

Empleado: (＿＿＿＿＿＿＿) ir en metro o en taxi.

Cliente: ¿Cuál es (＿＿＿＿＿＿＿) barato?

Empleado: El metro es más (＿＿＿＿＿＿＿) y más (＿＿＿＿＿＿＿).

D ¿Cómo dices lo siguiente? How do you say the following?

1 How can we get to Cuzco?   3 Can I pay by credit card?
2 Can I book a seat?   4 Can you smoke in the bus?

Check your answers.

LANGUAGE FOCUS

As well as the irregular verbs you have already seen, there is a further group of verbs in which the vowels change. For example, in **poder**, the **o** changes to **ue** in the present tense with the exception of the **nosotros/as** and **vosotros/as** forms.

poder to be able to (can)

yo	p**ue**do	*I can*
tú	p**ue**des	*you can*
usted	p**ue**de	*you can (formal)*
él/ella	p**ue**de	*he/she can*
nosotros/as	podemos	*we can*
vosotros/as	podéis	*you can*
ustedes	p**ue**den	*you can (formal)*
ellos/ellas	p**ue**den	*they can*

The verb **poder**, like *can* in English, has many uses, including:

• possibility   • permission

¿Cómo puedo ir al centro?
How can I go to the centre?

¿Puedo ir en tren o en autobús?
Can I go by train or by bus?

¿Puedo fumar aquí?
Can I smoke here?

7

LANGUAGE FOCUS

You have already met most of the basic question words. Here is a summary:

cómo	how	por qué	why
cuál	which	qué	what
cuándo	when	quién(es)	who
cuánto/a(s)	how many/much		
dónde	where	porque…	because…

In general, when you want to buy an underground, bus, coach, train or plane ticket, the vocabulary is the same wherever you are. The changes from country to country are very small. The most common are:

ticket
el billete (Spain)
el boleto (Latin America)

bus/coach
el autobús (Spanish)
el camión (Mexico)
la guagua (Cuba, Venezuela, Canary Islands)
la góndola (Peru)
el colectivo (Argentina)

car
coche (Spain)
carro (Latin America)

E ¿Cuántas preguntas puedes escribir usando los pronombres interrogativos? Comprueba con tu compañero/a.
How many questions can you write using the questions words? Check with a partner.

F Completa las preguntas. Complete the questions.

1 ¿ ( ) cuesta un billete de ida y vuelta para Guadalajara?

2 ¿ ( ) andén sale el próximo tren para Trinidad?

3 ¿ ( ) hora llega el autobús de Lugo?

4 ¿ ( ) puedo ir a Guadalupe?

5 ¿ ( ) puerta llega el vuelo de Nueva York?

G Escribe preguntas para las respuestas. Write questions for these answers.

1 Puedes ir en metro, en autobús o andando.

2 No, sólo aceptamos tarjetas de crédito.

3 Sí, tiene que bajar en la próxima estación.

4 Sale del andén catorce.

5 Llega a las cuatro menos cuarto.

6 No, aquí no se puede fumar.

7 Sí, tiene que reservar asiento, el tren va siempre lleno.

5 Preposiciones

LANGUAGE FOCUS

Prepositions are linking words which are usually placed before or between nouns to show the relationship between them. Spanish prepositions can have different meanings from English ones. Some of the most important prepositions are:

a

This common preposition has various meanings:

- *to* when referring to a destination:
  Quiero ir **a** la estación, por favor.　　　*I want to go to the station, please.*
- *at* when telling the time:
  a las seis y media　　　*at half past six*
- *away* when used with a distance:
  Está **a** seis kilómetros.　　　*It's six kilometres away.*

de

Another common preposition, **de** can be used:

- to mean *from* when referring to origins:
  Juan es **de** Barcelona.　　　*Juan is from Barcelona.*
- to mean *of* referring to content:
  un bocadillo **de** chorizo　　　*a chorizo sandwich*
- to indicate possession:
  El coche es **de** Carmina.　　　*The car is Carmina's.*
- to show what something is made of:
  unos guantes **de** piel　　　*some leather gloves*
- in expressions of time:
  de la tarde, **de** la mañana　　　*in the afternoon/morning*

hasta

This means *until* or *as far as*, either in place or time, with a sense of end:
Todo recto **hasta** el final de la calle.　　　*Straight ahead as far as the end of the street.*
hasta las cinco　　　*until five o'clock*

en

Be careful with this one, as it doesn't always translate as *in*:
El coche está **en** la plaza.　　　*The car is in the square.*
Mi bolso está **en** el coche.　　　*My bag is in the car.*
El libro está **en** la mesa.　　　*The book is on the table.*

UNIT **7**

ACCESS SPANISH

For more activities, go to our website
www.accesslanguages.com.

116

para

This has different meanings and can sometimes be confusing, but it generally means *for* or *in the direction of*:

Los calamares **para** mí.	*The squid for me.*
El vuelo IB381 sale **para** Bilbao.	*Flight IB381 is leaving for Bilbao.*

por

Like **para**, **por** has many meanings; the most common are *through* and *along*.

El tren de Sevilla pasa **por** Córdoba.	*The Seville train goes through Cordoba.*
Sigue recto **por** esta calle.	*Go straight ahead along this street.*

It is also used in many expressions:

por la mañana/tarde	*in the morning/evening*
por favor	*please*

desde

This means *from* or *since*:

desde aquí	*from here*	**desde** las dos *since two o'clock*

A Añade las preposiciones que faltan a estas frases.
Add the missing prepositions to these sentences. Listen and check.

1 El tren ⟨_____⟩ Salamanca tiene una hora de retraso y sale del andén 17.

2 Carmen es española, ⟨_____⟩ Sevilla.

3 Todos los alumnos están ⟨*están*⟩ la clase.

4 Me gustan las camisas ⟨*de*⟩ seda.

5 ¿Cómo se puede ir ⟨*da*⟩ Toledo?

6 Yo voy al colegio ⟨*en*⟩ metro.

7 Sale ⟨*a*⟩ las dos de la tarde.

8 ⟨*por*⟩ mí un vino tinto y ⟨*para*⟩ mi hijo un zumo ⟨*de*⟩ naranja.

9 Está ⟨*a*⟩ cinco minutos andando, siga todo recto ⟨*asta*⟩ el final ⟨*de*⟩ la calle.

10 El autobús ⟨*para*⟩ el centro pasa ⟨*por*⟩ la calle Arenal.

B  Estudia esta carta y rellena los huecos con las palabras del cuadro. Read this letter and fill in the gaps using the words in the box.

---

ocho y media   rápido

más   divertida   andando

tan   como   bonita

once y cinco   grande

hace   podemos (x 2)

desde   caro   te gustan

puedo (x 2)   directo

prefieres   te gusta

Now listen to the recording and check you got it right.

Sevilla, el 30 de junio

Querida Marina:

Lo siento, pero no puedo ir a verte. Ahora tengo mucho trabajo. ¿Por qué no vienes a visitarme? Sevilla es una ciudad muy (1) ⬭, simpática y (2) ⬭, no es muy (3) ⬭ y ahora (4) ⬭ buen tiempo.

Es muy fácil (5) ⬭ Madrid, toma el AVE, es el tren más (6) ⬭ que hay en España, sólo tarda dos horas y media y no es (7) ⬭ – ahora hay una oferta especial y un billete de ida y vuelta cuesta 99€. Hay otros trenes desde Madrid, pero son (8) ⬭ lentos. El TALGO es un tren rápido, pero no es (9) ⬭ rápido (10) ⬭ el AVE.

Mira, si tomas el tren a las (11) ⬭, puedes estar en Sevilla a las (12) ⬭. Yo no (13) ⬭ ir a recogerte, pero mi casa está muy cerca de la estación y puedes venir (14) ⬭ o tomar un autobús (15) ⬭.

Luego, por la mañana, (16) ⬭ ir a visitar la Isla Mágica, ahora con el billete de tren te regalan una entrada.

Por las tardes (17) ⬭ acompañarte a visitar la Giralda, la Torre del Oro y otros monumentos, o si (18) ⬭ podemos ir de compras y por las noches, si (19) ⬭ las tapas, (20) ⬭ ir de tapas y cenar fuera, luego ir de copas o ir a la discoteca si (21) ⬭ bailar.

Bueno, anímate y escribe pronto. Lo podemos pasar muy bien.

Un abrazo

Guillermo

READY
TO MOVE ON?

✓

Check that you can...

- enquire about available means of transport and how to get to places
- find out whether the journey is direct, whether you have to book a seat, etc.
- talk about travel in general and find out which means of transport is better
- use question words and prepositions

UNIT **7**

117

Descubre el mundo HISPANO

Rumbos del Perú

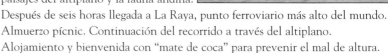

Itinerario

DÍA 01: ESPAÑA / LIMA

Salida a Lima, vía Caracas. Llegada y traslado al hotel. Alojamiento.

DÍA 02: LIMA / CUZCO

Desayuno en el hotel. Traslado al aeropuerto para salir en un vuelo a Cuzco.

Recepción en el aeropuerto de Cuzco y traslado al hotel.

Bienvenida con mate de hoja de coca. Por la tarde salida para visitar la ciudad y recorrido de algunas de las conocidas calles de Cuzco, como Hatunrumiyoq donde encontramos la Piedra de los doce ángulos. Por la noche cena espectáculo en un restaurante turístico.

DÍA 03: CUZCO / MACHU PICCHU/ CUZCO

Traslado a la estación del tren y salida hacia Aguas Calientes en un panorámico recorrido de tres horas y media de duración.

Traslado a la estacion de bus para ascender a la ciudadela de Machu Picchu (35 minutos). Visita guiada a la ciudadela. Regreso en autobús a Aguas Calientes. Almuerzo buffet. Regreso en tren a Cuzco.

DÍA 04: CUZCO / PUNO

Traslado a la estación de autobuses. Salida con destino a Puno. Durante el recorrido podrá observar los bellos paisajes del altiplano y la fauna andina. Después de seis horas llegada a La Raya, punto ferroviario más alto del mundo. Almuerzo pícnic. Continuación del recorrido a través del altiplano. Alojamiento y bienvenida con "mate de coca" para prevenir el mal de altura.

DIA 05: PUNO

Traslado al muelle para iniciar la excursión por el Titicaca, lago navegable más alto del mundo. La leyenda cuenta que de las aguas de este hermoso lago emergieron Manco Capac y Mama Ocllo para fundar el Imperio Inca.

DIA 06: PUNO / LIMA

Desayuno y traslado al aeropuerto de Juliaca. Llegada y traslado al hotel.

DIA 07: LIMA

Salida para visitar la ciudad: la Lima Colonial y Moderna, donde visitaremos la Plaz Mayor, con el Palacio de Gobierno, la catedral, la Municipalidad, la Iglesia de San Francisco y sus catacumbas.

DIA 08: LIMA / ESPAÑA

Traslado al aeropuerto, para salir con destino Madrid, vía Caracas. Noche a bordo.

DIA 09: ESPAÑA

Llegada. Fin del viaje.

A  Lee el itinerario de Perú y contesta las preguntas.
Read the itinerary for a holiday in Peru and answer the questions.

1   Haz una lista de los distintos medios de transporte que se usan en este itinerario.

2   Haz otra lista de los lugares que se visitan (ciudades y atracciones más interesantes).

3   ¿Cuál es en tu opinión la mejor atracción del itinerario?

B Di si las siguientes afirmaciones son verdaderas o falsas.
Say if the following statements are true or false.

1   Hatunrumiyoq es una de las calles más conocidas de Cuzco debido a sus ruinas.

2   Machu Picchu está a unos treinta y cinco minutos más o menos de Cuzco.

3   El "mate de coca" es una infusión que se toma como relajante.

4   La Raya es el lugar más alto del mundo al que se puede llegar en tren.

5   El lago navegable más alto del mundo es el lago Titicaca.

C Busca otros lugares y atracciones turísticas del Perú, puedes encontrar direcciones útiles en la página web.
Look for other Peruvian places and tourist attractions; our website has some useful links.

Un billete, por favor UNIT 7

119

GLOSSARY

Nouns

abril (m)	April
agosto (m)	August
andén (m)	platform
autobús (m)	bus, coach
avión (m)	plane
billete (m) (Sp)	ticket
boleto (m) (LA)	ticket
coche (m)	car
destino (m)	destination
día (m)	day
diciembre (m)	December
domingo (m)	Sunday
enero (m)	January
entrada (f)	(entrance) ticket
febrero (m)	February
jueves (m)	Thursday
julio (m)	July
junio (m)	June
llegada (f)	arrival
lunes (m)	Monday
martes (m)	Tuesday
marzo (m)	March
mayo (m)	May
mes (m)	month
miércoles (m)	Wednesday
monumento (m)	monument
noviembre (m)	November
octubre (m)	October
próximo/a (m/f)	next one
puerta (f)	gate, door
retraso (m)	delay
sábado (m)	Saturday
salida (f)	departure
semana (f)	week
septiembre (m)	September
tren (m)	train
vía (f)	platform
viernes (m)	Friday

Adjectives

cómodo/a	comfortable
rápido/a	fast, quick
último/a	last

Verbs

aterrizar	to land
llegar (a)	to reach, arrive/(at)
mirar	to look (at)
recoger	to meet, collect
salir (de)	to depart, leave
venir	to come
visitar	to visit

Prepositions

a	to
desde	from
hasta	until
por	for, through, along
vía	via, by way of

GLOSSARY

Others

ahora	now
hoy	today
mañana	tomorrow

Expressions

¿Cómo puedo ir a … ?	How can I go to …?
de ida	one way / single
de ida y vuelta	return
en punto	precisely, on the dot
¿Es directo?	Is it direct?
Es la una.	It's one o'clock.
(no) fumador	(non) smoking

menos cuarto	quarter to
por la mañana	in the morning
por la tarde	in the afternoon/evening
por la noche	at night
procedencia de	coming from
Son las …	It's … o'clock.
¿Tengo que bajar en …?	Do I have to get off in …?
¿Tengo que hacer transbordo?	Do I have to change?
y cuarto	quarter past
y media	half past

 # LOOKING FORWARD

In **Unit 8**, we will be looking at hotels and accommodation and learning how to make complaints.

Look at this letter and try to get as much information as you can. Use a dictionary if necessary

Hotel Cervantes
C/ Ancha, 19
Argamasilla de Alba, C. Real
Teléfono: 926 32 84 76
E-mail: hotelcervantes@terre.com

23 octubre 2004

Muy señores míos:

Les ruego reservarme una habitación doble con dos camas y una individual para tres noches a partir del 15 de noviembre próximo. Quiero las habitaciones con ducha, baño y aire acondicionado. ¿Puede confirmarme la reserva y el precio por noche? ¿Está el desayuno incluido? ¿Ofrecen media pensión?

En espera de sus noticias les saluda atentamente

Adso Peñasco
C/ Pablo Gargallo 34 1°A
Madrid

Quisiera una habitación

UNIT 7

UNIT 8
Quisiera una habitación

By the end of this unit you will be able to:

- Find and book a hotel room on the phone and by post
- Check in to a hotel
- Make a request
- Make a complaint
- Write a formal letter
- Describe your home

1 ¿Qué recuerdas?

A Escucha y rellena los cuadros con la información que oigas.

	Tipo de billete y destino	Clase	¿Cuándo? (hora/día)	Precio	Otra información
1	Ida y vuelta, Madrid	2	Esta tarde Sale a las 19:30 Llega a las 21:00	14€	
2					
3					
4					
5					

122

B 🎲 ▷ Pon estas instrucciones en orden.

1 Desde la plaza, toma la primera a la derecha, yo vivo en el número siete.

2 Para venir a mi casa desde el aeropuerto, toma el autobús al centro.

3 Bájate en la tercera parada.

4 Luego baja la calle hasta la plaza.

5 En el centro toma el autobús número 14.

There are two words for a hotel room in Spanish. You will usually hear **habitación** in Spain, but **cuarto** in Latin America.

In Spain, **el ascensor** is used to mean *lift*, but in Latin America, it is **el elevador**.

2 Una habitación doble con baño

▷ 👤 LANGUAGE FOCUS

The table below shows how to book a hotel.

Tengo reservada(s)

Quisiera Quiero	una dos		individual(es)						el jueves hoy
		habitación(es)	doble(s)	con	cama de matrimonio	con/sin	baño	para	esta noche
¿Tiene	tres				dos camas		ducha		el 15 de junio
¿Hay									una noche 🌙
									dos noches 🌙🌙
									tres noches 🌙🌙🌙

In Unit 5, you saw how to book a table in restaurant. You can use the same phrases to book a hotel room.

¿Tiene reservada una habitación?   *Have you booked a room?*

Tengo reservada una habitación.   *I have booked a room.*

¿Tiene una habitación libre?   *Have you got a room available?*

UNIT **8**

123

A Lee este correo electrónico (e-mail) y completa el diálogo.

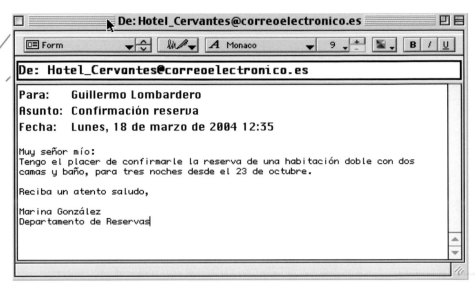

De: Hotel_Cervantes@correoelectronico.es

Para: Guillermo Lombardero
Asunto: Confirmación reserva
Fecha: Lunes, 18 de marzo de 2004 12:35

Muy señor mío:
Tengo el placer de confirmarle la reserva de una habitación doble con dos
camas y baño, para tres noches desde el 23 de octubre.

Reciba un atento saludo,

Marina González
Departamento de Reservas

Empleada: Buenos días.

Cliente: Buenos días, tengo

Empleada: Su nombre, por favor.

Cliente:

Empleada: ¿Cómo se escribe?

Cliente:

Empleada: Muy bien, señor. La reserva es para una habitación doble con cama de matrimonio, ¿verdad?

Cliente:

Empleada: ¿Y para cuántas noches?

Cliente:

Empleada: Su carnet de identidad, por favor.

Cliente: Aquí lo tiene.

Empleada: Habitación 346, en el segundo piso. Firme aquí, por favor.

Cliente: ¿Dónde, aquí?

Empleada: Sí. Su llave.

LEARNING TIP:
The **carnet** (**de identidad**) is an official identity card carried by all Spaniards. If you are asked for your **carnet**, you will need to supply a form of identification with your photo on, such as your passport.

B  Ahora escucha y comprueba (check).

C  Mira esta factura (bill) y lee la carta. Hay cuatro errores en la factura. Encuéntralos.

Hotel Cervantes ***
C/ Ancha, 19, Argamasilla de Alba, C. Real, España
Teléfono 926 32 84 76 **e.mail** hotelcervantes@terre.com

Sr. Rafael Peñasco
Fecha de llegada 15/10/04
Fecha de salida 17/10/04
Habitación número 469
Número de personas 2

	Día 15/10	Día 16/10	
Habitación	65€	65€	
Pensión alimenticia			
Desayuno			
Comida			
Cena			
Minibar			
Extras			Total
Firma del cliente			IVA

desayuno

comida

cena

pensión completa

media pensión

Hotel Cervantes
C/ Ancha, 19
Argamasilla de Alba
C. Real
23 octubre 2004

Muy señores míos:
Pueden reservarme una habitación individual para tres noches a partir del 15 de noviembre próximo.

Les saluda atentamente

Adso Peñasco
C/ Pablo Gargallo 34 1°A
Madrid

8

D Escucha estas conversaciones y rellena los cuadros.

	habitación individual/doble	con baño/ ducha	pensión media/ completa	no. noches	no. habitación	otra información
Cliente 1	*doble con cama de matrimonio*	*con baño*	■	*3*	■	
Cliente 2						
Cliente 3					■	
Cliente 4			■			

E Lee la información sobre el Hotel Meloneras. Intenta sacar la mayor información posible y, junto con tu compañero/a, hacer una lista de todos los servicios que proporciona el hotel. Luego contesta las preguntas. Look at this hotel brochure and try to get as much information as you can. With your partner, write a list of all the facilities provided, then answer the questions.

LEARNING TIP:
Ventajas are advantages. The opposite is **desventajas**.

1 ¿Cuántas habitaciones hay?
2 ¿Cómo son las habitaciones?
3 ¿Cuántos restaurantes hay?
4 ¿Qué tipo de menú tienen?

5 ¿Qué tipos de deportes puedes practicar?
6 ¿Tienen zona para niños?
7 ¿Qué otras ventajas puedes resaltar?

C/ Mar Mediterraneo, 1
Maspalomas 35100
España
1.136 Habitaciones

Gran Hotel Costa Meloneras ★ ★ ★ ★

Mas fotos

Descripción:
Habitaciones: con baño completo, ducha, secador de pelo, televisión vía satélite, teléfono, terraza con vistas, caja fuerte opcional y aire acondicionado. Instalaciones: cafetería, bar, recepción, aire acondicionado, piscina, sala de televisión, facilidades y habitaciones para minusválidos y servicio de lavandería. Restaurante: buffet.

Situación:
SITUACIÓN: En 1ª línea de mar, cerca de las dunas de Maspalomas. ALOJAMIENTO: Habitaciones con aire acondicionado, cuarto de baño completo con secador de pelo, TV. vía satélite, teléfono y terraza con vistas a la montaña. Habitación vistas piscina/jardin con suplemento. RESTAURACIÓN: Tres restaurantes con servicio a la carta. 5 bares, 1 cyber-café y 1 pub. INSTALACIONES Y ACTIVIDADES: Dispone de varios salones de convenciones y reuniones. 4 piscinas, con servicio de toallas, rodeadas de un amplio solarium con jacuzzi. Minuclub y zona de juegos para niños. Facilidades para la practica de paddle, con 2 pistas, y tenis, con 4 canchas. Amplio programa de entrenimiento y animación para adultos y niños durante el día, con shows y música en vivo por las noches. Descuentos en green fees en varios campos de golf. CARACTERISTICAS. INAUGURADO: En el 2004; Nº de habitaciones: 1.136. VIAJE DE NOVIOS: Botella de cava y ramo de flores. OBSERVACIONES: Gala de Navidad/Fin de Año: incluidas en el precio.

El hotel tiene los siguientes servicios:
Aire Acondicionado • Caja Fuerte • Deportes • Jacuzzi • Jardín/Terraza • Parque Infantil • Piscina • Piscina Climatizada • Restaurante • Salón de Reuniones • Sala de Juegos • Secador de Pelo • Solarium • Teléfono • Televisión • Tenis • Tiendas • TV satélite

F Compara los dos hoteles: Gran Hotel Costa Meloneras y AC Gran Canaria. Con tu compañero/a, escribe una lista de diferencias que hay entre ellos.

Eduardo Benot, 3
Las Palmas de Gran
Canaria 35007
España
227 Habitaciones

AC Gran Canaria ★ ★ ★ ★

Descripción:
Hotel totalmente reformado en el año 2001 para adaptarse a los cánones de calidad, diseño y confort de AC Hoteles. Dispone de 227 habitaciones distribuidas en 25 plantas, que constan de cuarto de baño completo, aire acondicionado, TV vía satélite y teléfono directo. Se completa con restaurante, cafetería, servicio de habitaciones, lavandería, sala de reuniones, sala fitness y piscina.

Situación:
En pleno centro de la capital de la Isla de Gran Canaria, muy cerca de la Playa de Las Canteras, Parque de Santa Catalina y del Puerto.

El hotel tiene los siguientes servicios:
Admite Tarjetas de Crédito • Aire Acondicionado • Ascensor • Bar/Cafetería • Dataport / Enchufe de Modem • Gimnasio • Habitaciones Nofumadores • Lavandería • Piscina • Restaurante • Salón de Reuniones • Sauna • Servicio Habitaciones 24 Horas • Teléfono • Teléfono Directo • Televisión • TV satélite

G Ahora con tu compañero/a trata de hacer tantas comparaciones como puedas, usando las formas del comparativo aprendidas. (Make as many comparatives as you can.)

Ejemplo: El hotel Costa Meloneras tiene más habitaciones que el hotel Gran Canaria.

Quisiera una habitación

Hotel Majestic

H ✍ 🔊 ▷ Haz preguntas a estas respuestas sobre el hotel AC Gran Canaria. (Write questions for these answers.)

1 Todas las habitaciones tienen cuarto de baño completo, aire acondicionado, TV vía satélite y teléfono directo.

2 Hay piscina, restaurante, salón de reuniones, sauna …

3 Tiene 227 habitaciones en 25 plantas.

4 Es Eduardo Benot, 3, Las Palmas de Gran Canaria 35007.

I ✍ ▷ Tu familia y tú queréis ir de vacaciones a España este verano. Escribe una carta a un hotel de tu elección reservando alojamiento para ti y tu familia. Solicita información sobre las instalaciones del hotel así como la zona.

You and your family would like to go on holiday to Spain this summer. Write a letter to a hotel, booking accommodation. Ask for information about the facilities at the hotel and the area.

READY
TO MOVE ON?

✓

Check that you can...

- book a room on the phone, by e-mail or by post
- write a letter confirming your reservatio
- check in and ask about facilities in the hotel

You'll find additional practice to help you with holiday accommodation on our website.

3 Permiso y quejas

Permission

You have already come across the expression **¿se puede?**, which is often used to say whether something is allowed or not.

¿Se puede fumar?	*Is smoking allowed?*
No **se puede** aparcar aquí.	*You can't park here.*

Complaints

There are several ways of saying that there's a problem or something isn't working:

- **No funciona ...**

No funciona	el ascensor.	*The lift*	*isn't working/is out of order.*
	la calefacción.	*The heating*	
	el aire acondicionado.	*The air conditioning*	
	la ducha.	*The shower*	
	la televisión.	*The TV*	

- **No hay ...**

No hay	agua caliente.	*There's no*	*hot water.*
	toallas.		*towels.*
	papel higiénico.		*toilet paper.*

- **... está(n)** + adjective

	Las sábanas **están sucias**.	*The sheets are dirty.*
	El baño **está sucio**.	*The bath is dirty.*
	La sopa **está fría**.	*The soup is cold.*
	El vino **está malo**.	*The wine is bad.*

A Mira las señales y escribe frases que las definan.
Write a sentence to describe each sign.

1   2   3   4   5

8

B Mira las imágenes y escribe frases que expresen el problema.

1

2

3

4

5

6

C Escucha estas cuatro conversaciones y escribe el problema.

D Estás en un hotel y estás disgustado/a con el servicio. Decides presentar una queja. Escribe tu queja en la hoja de reclamaciones.
You are in a hotel and you are not happy about the service. You decide to make a complaint.

Quiero quejarme de ...

E Lee el artículo sobre los paradores y escribe un resumen explicando qué son los paradores, dónde están situados y otras características.

Paradores turísticos revelan la historia de España

Recorrido Los paradores son paradas obligatorias de todo turista que viaje por tierras españolas. España posee un total de 85 construcciones históricas y monumentales que en la actualidad han sido convertidas en hoteles de gran prestigio.

Se encuentran situados por todo el país, siendo una muestra tangible del interés gubernamental por la recuperación de edificios históricos dándoles uso turístico, asentando zonas turísticas y atrayendo la iniciativa privada.

Es un modo diferente de dar acogida al turista, quien puede elegir entre una gran variedad de estilos de construcción y ambiente (los lujosos palacios renacentistas, castillos medievales o antiguos conventos).

Soñar con la imaginación Quienes aman soñar con vivir otras épocas, pueden hacer uso de la imaginación dentro de un ambiente repleto de tapices, decoración clásica, vegetación y arte. La cadena de paradores propone diversas rutas, unas más basadas en la tradición que otras, que recorren la Península Ibérica en todas sus vertientes.

Es así como se puede tomar la Ruta de la España Verde, desde las Rías Gallegas hasta los Pirineos; la Ruta de la Plata, que los romanos construyeron para unir el norte y el sur de España; el tradicional Camino de Santiago y la Ruta Pirenaica, entre otras posibles.

Huella imborrable Castillos, palacetes y conventos, llenos de una profunda riqueza histórica, hoy convertidos en Paradores de Turismo, esperan al viajero para darle una calurosa acogida y ofrecerle todas las comodidades y servicios de un hotel cinco estrellas.

Hospedaje Edificios históricos y monumentales

- Rutas manchegas: en la Ruta Castellano Manchega nace la morada encantada de Cuenca. Este parador fue en otros tiempos un convento. Resulta todo un lujo alojarse en este parador, desde el que se accede a las espectaculares Casas Colgadas por un puente que salva profundos desniveles.

- En la Ruta Castellana, Salamanca, ciudad de ciudades, tiene en su parador el balcón perfecto que osa asomarse a este prodigio de catedrales, plazas, monasterios y conventos.

- El nuevo Parador de Plasencia dedica especial atención a la gastronomía tradicional y a las actividades culturales y de naturaleza que se pueden desarrollar en la zona cercana al parador.

- Castillos: las fortalezas españolas son testigos mudos de batallas, conquistas y reconquistas de sus muchos héroes.

Paradores are government-run hotels. They are unusual in that they are situated in places which reflect Spain's history and culture, e.g. castles, palaces and monasteries. They usually offer a high standard of accommodation.

F Con tu compañero/a o en grupo cread un debate sobre qué tipo de alojamiento preferís y por qué. Usad el vocabulario del cuadro para ayudaros.

Discuss the type of accommodation you prefer and why.

hotel

parador

pensión

albergue juvenil

barato/a

caro/a

cómodo/a

elegante

más … que

tan … como

menos … que

Me gusta(n)

Prefiero

Me encanta(n)

Pienso que …

Creo que …

Tienes la oportunidad de conocer a otra gente, un lugar histórico…

Puedes estar en contacto con la naturaleza.

4 La vivienda

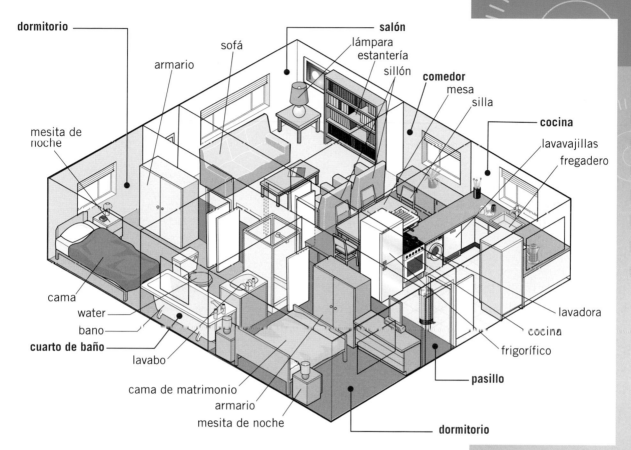

dormitorio
sofá
salón
lámpara
estantería
sillón
comedor
mesa
silla
armario
cocina
lavavajillas
fregadero
mesita de noche
mesita de noche
cama
water
baño
lavadora
cuarto de baño
cocina
frigorífico
lavabo
cama de matrimonio
armario
mesita de noche
pasillo
dormitorio

A Rellena los huecos con estos verbos. (**es** **está** **hay**)

1 En el comedor _____ una mesa.

2 El salón _____ enfrente del dormitorio.

3 La cocina _____ grande.

4 La cama _____ en el dormitorio.

5 _____ cuatro sillas en el comedor.

6 En el dormitorio _____ un armario pequeño.

7 El pasillo _____ vacío.

Listen and check.

Quisiera una habitación UNIT **8**

133

🎧 LANGUAGE FOCUS

nuestro/a, vuestro/a, su, nuestros/as, vuestros/as, sus

In Unit 3, you learned the words **mi padre**, **su hijo**, etc. to indicate relationship or ownership.

When there is a relationship with more than one person, you need the plural forms:

nuestro/nuestra	nuestros/nuestras	*our*
vuestro/vuestra	vuestros/vuestra	*your* (informal)
su	sus	*their / your* (formal)

As with the other possessives, they have to match the number and gender of the nouns they describe.

Nuestro hijo es muy alto pero nuestra hija no es alta.	Our son is very tall, but our daughter is not tall.
Vuestros zapatos son blancos y vuestras chaquetas negras.	Your shoes are white and your jackets are black

LEARNING TIP:

When you come to translate sentences 5 and 7 of activity 4B, you will realise that **su** and **sus** have many different meanings. Usually the context will make it clear which one it is, but you will sometimes see expressions added for clarity:

Nuestros uniformes están en su armario (**de él**).

B 🖊️ ◉ How would you say the following in English?

1 Nuestra casa es vieja y vuestro piso nuevo.

2 Nuestro libro está en la mesa en el comedor.

3 Los cuadernos están en vuestras habitaciones.

4 Nuestras hijas están en el dormitorio.

5 Nuestros uniformes están en su armario.

6 La llave está en nuestro cuarto.

7 Su hermano está en nuestra casa.

How would you say the following in Spanish?

8 Our books are on their table.

9 Your pens are in our bags.

10 The map is on the wall.

C Identifica al dueño, respondiendo a las preguntas.
Identify who the following items belong to by answering the questions.

Ejemplo: ¿De quién es la llave?   (vosotros) → Es vuestra llave.

1 ¿De quién es el dormitorio? (vosotros)

2 ¿De quién es el piso? (él)

3 ¿De quién es el sillón? (yo)

4 ¿De quién es la cama? (nosotros)

5 ¿De quién es la estantería? (tú)

6 ¿De quién es la habitación? (ella)

7 ¿De quién es el coche? (Carmen y Juan)

8 ¿De quién es la casa? (ellos)

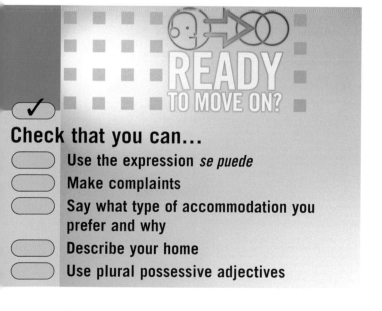

Check that you can...

- Use the expression *se puede*
- Make complaints
- Say what type of accommodation you prefer and why
- Describe your home
- Use plural possessive adjectives

For more activities in this unit, go to our website: www.accesslanguages.com

Quisiera una habitación UNIT 8

Descubre el mundo HISPANO

México desconocido

A ¿Conoces México? Haz una lista de diez palabras relacionadas con México.

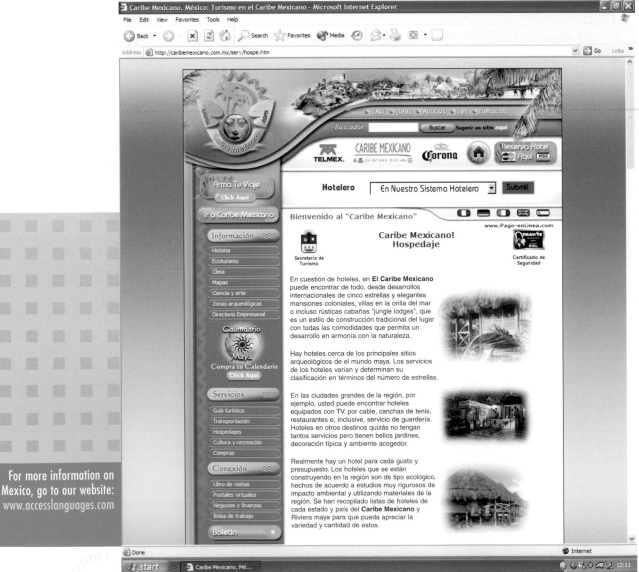

Caribe Mexicano, México: Turismo en el Caribe Mexicano - Microsoft Internet Explorer

File   Edit   View   Favorites   Tools   Help

Back   Search   Favorites   Media

Address   http://caribemexicano.com.mx/serv/hospe.htm

Buscador   Buscar   Sugerir un sitio **aqui**

TELMEX   CARIBE MEXICANO   Corona   Reserva Hotel Aqui

Hotelero   En Nuestro Sistema Hotelero   Submit

Bienvenido al "Caribe Mexicano"   www.Pago-enLinea.com

Caribe Mexicano!
Hospedaje

Secretaría de Turismo   Certificado de Seguridad

En cuestión de hoteles, en **El Caribe Mexicano** puede encontrar de todo, desde desarrollos internacionales de cinco estrellas y elegantes mansiones coloniales, villas en la orilla del mar o incluso rústicas cabañas "jungle lodges", que es un estilo de construcción tradicional del lugar con todas las comodidades que permita un desarrollo en armonía con la naturaleza.

Hay hoteles cerca de los principales sitios arqueológicos de el mundo maya. Los servicios de los hoteles varían y determinan su clasificación en términos del número de estrellas.

En las ciudades grandes de la región, por ejemplo, usted puede encontrar hoteles equipados con TV. por cable, canchas de tenis, restaurantes e, inclusive, servicio de guardería. Hoteles en otros destinos quizás no tengan tantos servicios pero tienen bellos jardines, decoración típica y ambiente acogedor.

Realmente hay un hotel para cada gusto y presupuesto. Los hoteles que se están construyendo en la región son de tipo ecológico, hechos de acuerdo a estudios muy rigurosos de impacto ambiental y utilizando materiales de la región. Se han recopilado listas de hoteles de cada estado y país del **Caribe Mexicano** y Riviera maya para que pueda apreciar la variedad y cantidad de estos.

Arma Tu Viaje   Click Aqui

Ir a Caribe Mexicano

Información
Historia
Ecoturismo
Clima
Mapas
Ciencia y arte
Zonas arqueológicas
Directorio Empresarial

Calendario Maya
Compra tu Calendario   Click Aqui

Servicios
Guía turística
Transportación
Hospedajes
Cultura y recreación
Compras

Conexión
Libro de visitas
Postales virtuales
Negocios y finanzas
Bolsa de trabajo

Boletín

Done   Internet

start   Caribe Mexicano, Mé...   12:11

B (A C) ◐ Di si las siguientes afirmaciones son verdaderas o falsas.

1 Los hoteles de cinco estrellas son mansiones coloniales.

2 Las cabañas rústicas son típicas de la zona.

3 Los servicios de los hoteles varían según la categoría del hotel.

4 En las ciudades los hoteles tienen más comodidades que en las zonas menos pobladas y sus jardines son mejores.

5 Los hoteles en construcción tratan de estar en armonía con el lugar.

꒰ᯤ꒱El ecoturismo en México

¿Qué es Ecoturismo?

Existen diferentes definiciones, pero todas deberían tener en cuenta estos criterios:

1 proveer medidas para la conservación

2 incluir una verdadera participación de las comunidades indígenas

3 debe ser rentable y mantenerse por sí mismo

México cuenta con gran potencial para el desarrollo del ecoturismo. Existen en el país alrededor de 93 Áreas Nacionales Protegidas decretadas (existen otras en proceso de designar) que cubren una extensión territorial de 11.8 millones de hectáreas. Esto es equivalente al 6% del territorio nacional.

El ecoturismo en la Península del Yucatán

Conozcamos la Península de Yucatán desde la selva hasta el Caribe. Realizando un recorrido a través de las pequeñas cabañas del mundo maya y explorando las pirámides y santuarios de hace 1,500 años, en un hábitat protegido que cuenta con aves, monos y una amplia diversidad vegetal y animal. Además también podemos descubrir el mundo maravilloso de los ríos subterráneos en la Península, los 'cenotes'; así como disfrutar de las blancas arenas y el mar azul turquesa del Caribe mexicano.

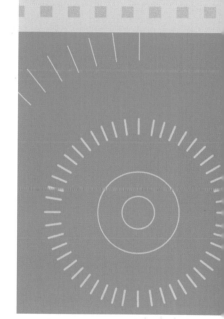

Quisiera una habitación

8

C ✎ ▷ Escribe en inglés una definición para 'ecoturismo'.

D [A▢] ▷ Pon en orden estas frases de tal forma que formen un resúmen sobre el segundo párafo del texto anterior, siguiendo el orden.
Put these sentences in order so that they form a summary of the second paragraph of the text above.

El ecoturismo en la Península del Yucatán

a así como gozaremos de las blancas arenas y el mar azul turquesa del Caribe mexicano.

b Haciendo un trayecto por la civilización maya

c Conozcamos este lugar desde la jungla hasta el mar.

d en un medio protegido que cuenta una amplia diversidad de flora y fauna,

e también descubriremos los ríos subterráneos de la Península,

f y recorriendo minuciosamente sus ruinas y antiguos monumentos

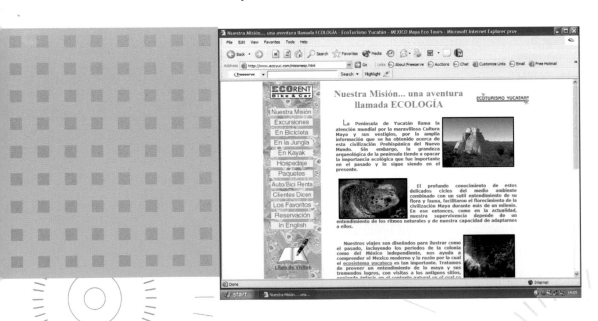

GLOSSARY

Nouns

agua (f)	water
aire acondicionado (m)	air conditioning
albergue juvenil (m)	youth hostel
ascensor (m) (Sp)	lift
asunto (m)	subject
baño (m)	bath
cadena (f)	chain
calefacción (f)	heating
cama (f)	bed
cama de matrimonio (f)	double bed
carnet (de identidad) (m)	identity card
cocina (f)	kitchen; cooker
comedor (m)	dining room
correo electrónico (m)	e-mail
cuarto (m)	room
cuarto de baño (m)	bathroom
dormitorio (m)	bedroom
ducha (f)	shower
elevador (m) (LA)	lift
estantería (f)	shelves
factura (f)	bill, invoice
fecha (f)	date
fregadero (m)	(kitchen) sink
habitación (f)	room
instalaciones (fpl)	facilities
lámpara (f)	lamp
lavabo (m)	washbasin
lavadora (f)	washing machine
lavavajillas (m)	dishwasher
libro de reclamaciones (m)	complaints book

mesilla de noche (f)	bedside table
mini-bar (m)	minibar
papel higiénico (m)	toilet paper
pasillo (m)	corridor
placer (m)	pleasure
restaurante (m)	restaurant
salón (m)	living room
salón de reuniones (m)	meeting room
servicios (mpl)	services; toilets
silla (f)	chair
sillón (m)	armchair
sofá (m)	sofa
televisión (f)	TV
toalla (f)	towel
vaso (m)	glass
wáter (m)	toilet

Adjectives

caliente	hot
doble	double
elegante	elegant
frío/a	cold
individual	single
nuestro/a	our
sucio/a	dirty
vuestro/a	your

Verbs

conocer	to know, meet, get to know
firmar	to sign
solicitar	to ask for

Quisiera una habitación UNIT 8

GLOSSARY

Expressions

Creo que …	I believe/think that …
media pensión	half board
pensión completa	full board
Pienso que …	I think that …

 # LOOKING FORWARD

In **Unit 9**, we will be talking about how often you do things, daily routine, where to go on holiday and other plans.

To prepare, look at these pictures

levantarse

ducharse

vestirse

desayunar

ir a trabajar

comer

volver a casa

ver la tele

cenar

acostarse

UNIT 9 La rutina diaria

UNIT 9
La rutina diaria

By the end of this unit you will be able to:

- Say how often you do things
- Describe your daily routine
- Describe your weekends
- Talk about things you love to do
- Talk about where you are going on holiday and other plans

1 ¿Qué recuerdas?

A Un amigo tuyo quiere alquilar (rent) un apartamento en España en julio. Él ha leído este anuncio (advert) en una revista, y quiere hacerte algunas preguntas sobre el anuncio. Contesta en español.

1 How many rooms are there?

2 Is it far from the beach?

3 Are there any shopping facilities in the area?

4 What facilities are available?

5 Is the city centre accessible?

LEARNING TIP:

se alquila	to let
se vende	for sale
se compra	wanted (to buy)/ we buy

UNIT

9

Please phone the Almagro Parador and book a double room for my boss Mr Doughty and his wife. They will be arriving in Almagro on 1st July and will be staying there for the weekend.

B 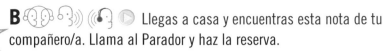 Llegas a casa y encuentras esta nota de tu compañero/a. Llama al Parador y haz la reserva.

You arrive home and find the following note. Phone the Parador and make the booking. Your partner can play the receptionist's role.

Recepcionista: Buenos días, Parador de Almagro, ¿dígame?

Tú:

Recepcionista: ¿La quiere individual o doble?

Tú:

Recepcionista: ¿Para cuántas noches?

Tú:

Recepcionista: ¿Desde cuándo?

Tú:

Recepcionista: Lo siento, pero el parador está completo ese fin de semana.

Tú: *Ask if he/she can recommend another parador or hotel in the area.*

Recepcionista: Es el 1 de julio y muchos españoles empiezan sus vacaciones de verano, va a ser muy difícil encontrar habitación para ese fin de semana.

Tú: *Ask what you can do.*

Recepcionista: Sólo queda una habitación individual, la habitación es grande y podemos poner una cama supletoria, si lo desea.

Tú: *Say you are going to check with your friend and you will phone back straight away.*

Recepcionista: Muy bien, hasta ahora.

Tú:

C Une (Match) las palabras en la columna derecha con los adjetivos y palabras de la columna izquierda para formar frases completas.

1	La casa es	a	piscina, jardín y muchas otras cosas.
2	Las habitaciones tienen	b	cerca de la playa.
3	Las habitaciones son	c	grande y moderna.
4	El hotel tiene	d	muy cómodas.
5	El piso es	e	aire acondicionado, calefacción, televisión.
6	La casa está	f	pequeño y antiguo.

2 Todos los días

A  Mira esta 'foto' de Elena. Pon esta historia en orden. Usa el diccionario si tienes problemas con el significado de algunos de los verbos.

a A las nueve de la tarde terminan las clases y vuelvo a casa.

b Me levanto a las dos y media, me ducho y me visto.

c Ceno, estudio y preparo las clases del día siguiente.

d A las cinco empiezan las clases en la universidad.

e Trabajo toda la noche.

f A las once y media me pongo el uniforme y salgo para el trabajo.

g Llego a casa a las siete más o menos; tomo un chocolate caliente y me acuesto.

h Luego como y veo la tele, escucho música o leo el periódico.

B Escucha y comprueba tu respuesta.

C Habla con tu compañero/a.

1 ¿Qué horario de trabajo tiene Elena?

2 ¿Qué creéis (think) que estudia?

3 ¿Por qué?

D Mira estos verbos y clasifícalos en tres grupos según sus terminaciones.

-ar	-er	-ir

Ahora clasifícalos en regulares e irregulares.

LEARNING TIP:

Note that some of the verbs are reflexive. The **se** on the end is a pronoun. (See page 144.)

> **despertarse** (to wake up)
> **levantarse   ducharse**
> **vestirse   desayunar   ir**
> **empezar   comer**
> **terminar   volver**
> **ver   preparar**
> **cenar   escuchar**
> **lavarse   acostarse**
> **dormirse** (to fall asleep)

La rutina diaria

LANGUAGE FOCUS

Daily routine

To refer to daily activities or habitual activities, verbs are normally used in the present tense.

Todos los días **como** a las dos y media y **estudio** por la tarde. A veces **voy** al cine.

*Every day **I have lunch** at half past two and **I study** in the afternoon. Sometimes **I go** to the cinema.*

Reflexive verbs

In the infinitive, these are shown by adding **se** to the end of the verb.

However, the reflexive pronoun changes, depending on the subject: llamar**se** → **Me** llamo Eva.

In English, some verbs can be used with or without the reflexive pronoun without changing their meaning. For example, *Every day I wash myself* or *Every day I wash* mean pretty much the same thing. However, in Spanish this flexibility does not exist, so you must always use **se**.

Todos los días **me levanto** y **me lavo**, luego **levanto** y **lavo** a mi bebé.

Every day I get up and I wash (myself), then I get my baby up and wash him/her.

Irregular verbs

There are a number of irregular verbs in Spanish. Some are irregular in the first person singular.

salir → **Salgo** a las ocho y media de la mañana.

Others change in the middle (the stem).

empezar (to start) → Emp**ie**zo a trabajar a las nueve de la mañana.

Some have both irregularities

tener → Siempre **tengo** mucho trabajo porque el Sr. Doughty t**ie**ne demasiadas responsabilidades.

3 La rutina de Alejandra

A 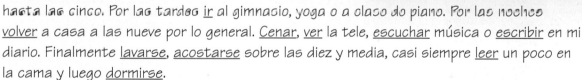 Corrige el texto y cambia los infinitivos de los verbos <u>subrayados</u> pon su forma correcta en presente de indicativo. No olvides que algunos son irregulares y otros reflexivos.

Hola, me llamo Alejandra, vivo en Lima y trabajo en un tribunal. Soy la secretaria del señor Doughty. Siempre tengo mucho trabajo, por eso mi vida es muy ordenada.

Durante la semana <u>despertarse</u> a las ocho menos cuarto, <u>levantarse</u> a las ocho más o menos, <u>ducharse</u>, <u>vestirse</u>, <u>desayunar</u> y <u>salir</u> de casa sobre las ocho y media. <u>Tomar</u> el metro y <u>llegar</u> al trabajo a las nueve. <u>Trabajar</u> toda la mañana y <u>salir</u> a comer a la una. Normalmente <u>comer</u> en la cafetería con algún compañero, <u>volver</u> a la oficina a las dos y <u>trabajar</u> hasta las cinco. Por las tardes <u>ir</u> al gimnasio, yoga o a clase de piano. Por las noches <u>volver</u> a casa a las nueve por lo general. <u>Cenar</u>, <u>ver</u> la tele, <u>escuchar</u> música o <u>escribir</u> en mi diario. Finalmente <u>lavarse</u>, <u>acostarse</u> sobre las diez y media, casi siempre <u>leer</u> un poco en la cama y luego <u>dormirse</u>.

B  Escribe cinco preguntas sobre Alejandra y su rutina. Haz las preguntas a tu compañero/a y responde a sus preguntas.

¿Dónde trabaja?

C Escucha ahora a Alejandra describiendo su rutina a una amiga, y di qué diferencias hay entre el texto de la actividad 3A y lo que ella cuenta.

Trabaja en un tribunal.

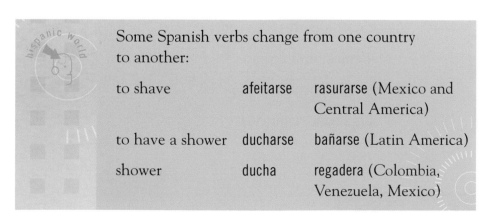

Some Spanish verbs change from one country to another:

to shave	afeitarse	rasurarse (Mexico and Central America)
to have a shower	ducharse	bañarse (Latin America)
shower	ducha	regadera (Colombia, Venezuela, Mexico)

D 🔍 ⓓ Ordena estas frases para que tengan sentido.

1 levanto las me ocho mañanas a todas las

2 empiezan mis estudiar amigos español a este año

3 duchamos por normalmente nos noches las

4 duerme se música con siempre

5 terminamos a trabajar de nueve las

6 salgo la sobre oficina de cinco más o menos las

E 🔤 ⓓ Busca las expresiones siguientes en el texto de la actividad 3A y escribe su significado en inglès.

1 siempre   **2** casi siempre   **3** normalmente   **4** por lo general   **5** finalmente

F 🔍 ⓓ Piensa qué haces tú normalmente y escribe un párrafo similar a la actividad 3A.

G 🔍 ⓓ Imagina que eres Alejandra y trabajas en el despacho del señor Doughty. Explica tu trabajo diario en el despacho (office); para ello usa las expresiones de frecuencia y el vocabulario siguiente.

> **Mirar el correo electrónico**
>
> **Consultar la agenda**
>
> **Planear el día de mi jefe**
>
> **Clasificar la correspondencia**
>
> **Contestar el correo**
>
> **Realizar las llamadas telefónicas**
>
> **Organizar reuniones**

H 🎧 ▶ Escucha a estas cuatros personas hablando de lo que hacen todos los días y di a cuál de las fotos corresponde cada diálogo.

A

B

C

D

READY
TO MOVE ON?

Check that you can...
- describe your daily routine and habits
- say how often you do things
- relate a sequence of events

9

4 Está de moda echarse la siesta

Se está convirtiendo en una verdadera revolución que traspasa nuestras fronteras ...

Panorama

R E P O R T A J E S

Los alemanes rompen el mito español al ser los europeos que más siestas echan

Texto:
Fermín Apezteguia. Bilbao

Los especialistas coinciden en que la siesta, bien echada, es muy beneficiosa para el organismo

A los médicos les cuesta creerlo, pero lo dicen las encuestas. Los europeos que más duermen la siesta no son españoles, ni portugueses, sino alemanes. Es más: hasta los ingleses se echan más cabezaditas después de comer que sus vecinos del sur de Europa. Parece increíble, pero es cierto. Aun así, los expertos dudan. «No me cuadra mucho, porque donde la costumbre está más extendida es en los lugares donde más calor hace. Por eso en Málaga se estila más que en el País Vasco, pero... ¿en Alemania más que en España, Italia o Grecia...?», se pregunta Javier Zamacona, médico adjunto del servicio de Neurofisiología Clínica del hospital vizcaíno de Cruces.

A Lee el artículo y contesta estas preguntas.

1 ¿Quiénes son los europeos que más duermen la siesta?

2 ¿En qué provincias españolas se echa más gente la siesta?

3 Según el artículo, ¿crees que el calor influye a la hora de echarse la siesta?

B (((🎧))) (▶) Ahora escucha el programa de radio sobre la siesta y di si estas afirmaciones son verdaderas o falsas.

	verdadera	falsa

1 La hora de la siesta es la parte del día en la que hace más calor.

2 La siesta es un período de descanso.

3 La comida tiene como objetivo: dividir el día, reponer la mente y prepararse para el trabajo de la tarde.

4 Muchos españoles dedican entre quince y treinta minutos a dar una cabezada en un sillón.

5 En invierno, por el frío, adultos y niños se acuestan (en la cama).

6 En verano, en los sitios donde hace mucho calor, los adultos y los niños se acuestan o se echan en un sofá o una hamaca (deckchair) en el patio o en la playa.

La rutina diaria UNIDAD **9**

5 ¿Qué haces los fines de semana?

LANGUAGE FOCUS

Plural reflexive pronouns

The reflexive pronouns in the plural are as follows:

Nos Nosotros **nos** levantamos muy temprano y **nos** vestimos.
We get up very early and get dressed.

Os Vosotros **os** acostáis demasiado tarde y **os** dormís enseguida.
You go to bed too late and fall asleep at once.

Se Ellos **se** levantan siempre los primeros y **se** visten los últimos.
They always get up first and get dressed last.

A 🎲 ✏️ 🎧 ▷ Los fines de semana son distintos para Alejandra. Ella pasa el fin de semana con su novio. Lee el texto y rellena los huecos con el verbo apropiado (no olvides conjugarlo).

> salir (x 2)   cenar   comer   ir (x 5)
> descansar   ser   levantarse (x 2)
> volver (x 2)   arreglarse   escuchar
> soler   leer   ver   acostarse   tomar

LEARNING TIP:

The verb **soler** is very useful. It means *to usually do something / be in the habit of doing something.* Be careful, as its stem changes:

Suelo dormir ocho horas.
I usually sleep for eight hours.

¿Sueles salir los sábados por la noche?
Do you usually go out on Saturday nights?

Solemos ir a Francia en verano.
We usually go to France in the summer.

Para mí, los fines de semana empiezan los viernes por la tarde.

Después de trabajar quedo con mi novio, (1) ( ) al teatro, (2) ( ) de copas con nuestros amigos o (3) ( ) fuera. Los sábados (4) ( ) temprano y (5) ( ) a algún mercadillo, en Lima hay tantos que nunca (6) ( ) al mismo, después (7) ( ) el aperitivo. A veces en invierno (8) ( ) a galerías de arte, museos o exposiciones. Por las tardes (9) ( ) a casa y (10) ( ). Luego (11) ( ) y (12) ( ) a cenar con amigos, y por la noche (13) ( ) ir a la discoteca. Me encanta bailar.

Los domingos (14) (_____) más relajados; (15) (_____)
tarde, (16) (_____) el periódico, (17) (_____) en algún bar y
siempre (18) (_____) al cine por la tarde. Después (19) (_____)
a casa, (20) (_____) la tele o (21) (_____) música pero
siempre (22) (_____) temprano.

Listen and check your answers.

B ✎ ▷ Escribe una pregunta para cada respuesta de Alejandra sobre sus
actividades los fines de semana.

1 *¿Cuándo empieza el fin de semana para ti?*

El fin de semana empieza el viernes por la tarde.

2 ¿ (_____) ?

El sábado por la mañana me levanto temprano y
voy al mercadillo.

3 ¿ (_____) ?

Salimos a cenar con amigos y vamos a la discoteca.

4 ¿ (_____) ?

Los domingos comemos en un restaurante.

5 ¿ (_____) ?

Siempre vamos al cine.

6 ¿ (_____) ?

Nos acostamos temprano.

C 🗣 👥 ▷ Mira estas expresiones y con tu compañero/a trata de explicar
su significado.

1 ir de vinos   **2** ir de copas   **3** comer fuera   **4** cenar fuera   **5** tomar el aperitivo

D 🗣 ▷ Con la ayuda de tu compañero/a une estas expresiones con su traducción
correspondiente en inglés.

1	a menudo	**a**	once, twice (a week/month)
2	a veces	**b**	often
3	una vez, dos veces (por semana / al día)	**c**	sometimes
4	de vez en cuando	**d**	never
5	nunca	**e**	from time to time

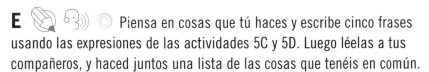

E Piensa en cosas que tú haces y escribe cinco frases usando las expresiones de las actividades 5C y 5D. Luego léelas a tus compañeros, y haced juntos una lista de las cosas que tenéis en común.

F Otras actividades para los fines de semana.

Estudia las tres columnas y forma todas las expresiones posibles uniendo la primera columna con las otras dos. (Recuerda: no siempre tienes que usar la columna del medio.)

ir	a	aperitivo
hacer	de	cine
tomar	al	copas
cenar	la	compra
comer	el	exposiciones
		deporte
		compras
		fuera
		teatro
		correr

G A estas frases les falta una preposición: **a**, **en**, **de**, **por** o **para**. Corrígelas.

1 ¿Qué haces los fines de semana ⟨ ⟩ la tarde?

2 ¿A qué hora terminas ⟨ ⟩ trabajar?

3 ¿Trabajas ⟨ ⟩ un despacho?

4 ¿Te levantas temprano ⟨ ⟩ ir a trabajar?

5 ¿Vas muy a menudo ⟨ ⟩ la piscina?

6 ¿Cuándo empiezas ⟨ ⟩ trabajar?

7 ¿Adónde vas los sábados ⟨ ⟩ la noche?

8 ¿Cuándo sales ⟨ ⟩ viaje?

6 Me encanta la música

encantar

When you love doing something, you say: **Me encanta ...** or **Me encantan ...**
Encantar follows the same rules as **gustar**, so the verb agrees with the thing you love.

Me **encanta** la música.	*I love music.*
Me **encantan** las películas españolas.	*I love Spanish films.*
Me **encanta** ver películas españolas.	*I love watching Spanish films.*

A Completa la tabla.

me encanta / me encantan   I love

te encanta / te ( )   you love

le ( ) / le encantan   he/she ( ) / you ( )

( ) ( ) / nos ( )   We ( )

( ) ( ) / ( ) ( )   ( )

( ) ( ) / ( ) ( )   ( )

B Rellena los huecos con la forma adecuada del verbo **encantar** y el pronombre correspondiente.

1 A Juan ( ) el cine.

2 A mí ( ) la música clásica.

3 A nosotros ( ) el deporte.

4 A Ricardo y Antonio ( ) las películas de ciencia-ficción.

5 A Maite ( ) los conciertos de música clásica.

6 A ti ( ) los deportes de invierno.

7 A vosotros ( ) comer en restaurantes caros.

C ✏️ 🎧 ▷ Di este diálogo en español.

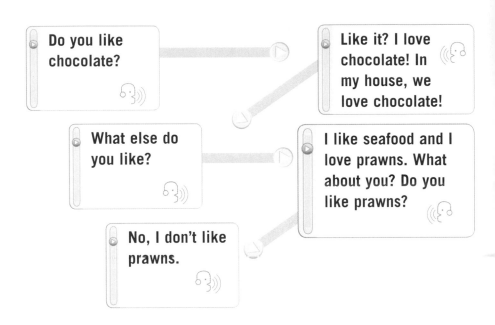

Do you like chocolate?

Like it? I love chocolate! In my house, we love chocolate!

What else do you like?

I like seafood and I love prawns. What about you? Do you like prawns?

No, I don't like prawns.

D 🗣️ 👥 ▷ Junto con tu compañero/a, contesta estas preguntas.

1 ¿Qué te gusta hacer los fines de semana?

2 ¿Qué es lo que más te gusta de todo?

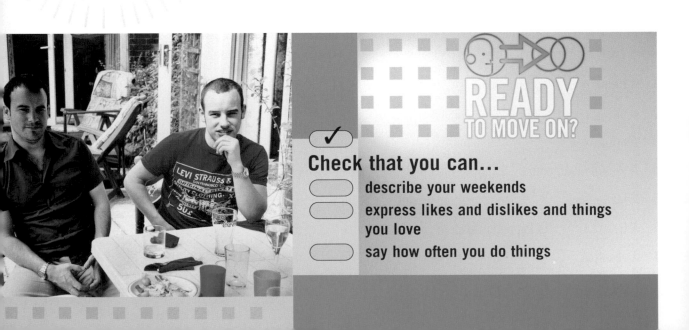

READY TO MOVE ON?

✔

Check that you can...

describe your weekends

express likes and dislikes and things you love

say how often you do things

7 ¿Adónde vas a ir de vacaciones?

LANGUAGE FOCUS

ir a

You've already learnt that **ir** is often used with the preposition **a + el/la** and a destination to tell you where people are going or to make suggestions:

Vamos a la tienda.   *Let's go to the shop.*
Voy al mercado.   *I am going to the market.*

Remember the contractions when followed by a noun:
a + el   – al
de + el = del

Ir a can also be followed by an infinitive to express future plans or say what is going to happen:

yo	**voy**	
tú	**vas**	
usted/él/ella	**va**	**a** + infinitive
nosotros/as	**vamos**	
vosotros/as	**vais**	
ustedes/ellos/ellas	**van**	

Mañana **voy a jugar** al fútbol.
*Tomorrow **I am going to play** football.*

A Mira la agenda de Carmen y escribe una lista de las cosas que va a hacer la semana próxima (next week).

LUNES
◎   *10:30 Examen de matemáticas*   *20:00 Cine Astoria "Terminator 2"*

MARTES
◎   *12:30 Comida con Victoria en*   *16:00 Dr. Loredo*
     el restaurante "el Caldero"

MIÉRCOLES
◎   *9:00 Examen de inglés*

JUEVES
◎   *11:15 Gimnasio*   *Fiesta de cumpleaños de Carmen*

VIERNES
◎   *18:00 Exposición Picasso*   *20:00 Cena con Carlos*

SÁBADO
◎   *22:00 Concierto "Los Intocables"*

DOMINGO
◎   *Excursión a la sierra con Carmen y Carlos*

LEARNING TIP:

¡Vamos a ver!   Let's see!
Vamos a hablar.   Let's talk.

Have a look at what Spanish people do at the weekend.

El lunes por la mañana va a tener un examen de matemáticas.
Por la tarde va a ver "Terminator 2" en el cine Astoria.

UNIT **9**

155

To talk about future plans or what is going to happen in the future, use these expressions:

mañana	tomorrow
pasado mañana	the day after tomorrow
la semana próxima / la semana que viene	next week
el mes próximo / el mes que viene	next month
el año próximo / el año que viene	next year

Notice that **mañana** has two meanings. As well as *morning* it can also mean *tomorrow*.

Está mañana hace frío.
It is cold this morning.

Mañana va a hacer frío.
Tomorrow is going to be cold.

mañana por la mañana
tomorrow morning

B ✎ ○ Escribe frases en la forma **ir a** …

Ejemplo: Mañana voy a comprar un regalo para mi tío Eugenio.

1

2

3

4

5

6

7

C Rellena los huecos con el presente del verbo **ir**.

Concha: Félix, ¿adónde (1) _____ a ir de vacaciones?

Félix: Este año (2) _____ a ir a la playa.

Concha: ¿Con quién (3) _____ a ir?

Félix: (4) _____ a ir con mis amigos.

Concha: Y tú, ¿cómo (5) _____ a viajar?

Félix: (6) _____ a viajar en avión.

Concha: ¿Qué (7) _____ a hacer allí?

Félix: Por las mañanas (8) _____ a tomar el sol y (9) _____ a nadar en el mar.

Concha: ¿Y por las tardes?

Félix: Por las tardes mis amigos y yo (10) _____ a jugar al tenis.

Concha: ¿Dónde (11) _____ a dormir tus amigos y tú?

Félix: (12) _____ a dormir en un camping en la playa.

Concha: ¿(13) _____ a hacer excursiones juntos?

Félix: No sé, creo que sí (14) _____ a hacer algunas. ¿Quieres venir con nosotros?

Concha: No puedo, (15) _____ a ir con mis padres de vacaciones a México y ya tienen los billetes.

Félix: ¡Qué pena!

D Ahora escucha y comprueba.

E Imagina que eres Félix y escribe una carta a un amigo diciéndole lo que vas a hacer este verano.

La rutina diaria 9

F Lee este itinerario y escucha la grabación. Un guía turístico da la bienvenida a su grupo y les explica lo que van a hacer durante las próximas dos semanas. ¿Qué cambios hay en el itinerario?

E GUATEMALA A COSTA RICA

1 ESPAÑA - GUATEMALA Presentación en el aeropuerto de Madrid Barajas 2 horas antes de la salida del vuelo y traslado al hotel. Alojamiento.

2 GUATEMALA Desayuno americano en el hotel y día libre. No dejen de visitar el Centro Histórico de la Ciudad.

3 GUATEMALA - CHICHICASTENANGO Desayuno en el hotel. Salida en tour regular para visitar la zona arqueológica del Baul y la Democracia. Continuación hacia Chichicastenango, llegada y alojamiento.

4 CHICHICASTENANGO - QUETZALTENANGO Después del desayuno, visita al colorido mercado al aire libre. Y a la Iglesia de Santo Tomás, de 1540, donde los ritos católicos se mezclan con los de origen maya. Por la tarde continuaremos hacia Quetzaltenango. Llegada y alojamiento.

5 QUETZALTENANGO - LAGO DE ATITLAN Desayuno. Visita del colorido mercado de animales de San Francisco El Alto, y visita a la Iglesia de San Andrés Xecul. Por la tarde traslado al Lago Atitlán. Alojamiento.

6 LAGO ATITLAN - ANTIGUA Desayuno en el hotel. Visita en lancha al pintoresco pueblo de Santiago de Atitlan. Por la tarde salida hacia Antigua. Llegada y alojamiento.

7 ANTIGUA - GUATEMALA - SAN JOSE Desayuno americano en el hotel y visita de la ciudad de Antigua, capital colonial española. Por la tarde traslado al aeropuerto de Guatemala. Salida del vuelo y traslado al hotel. Alojamiento.

8 SAN JOSE - TORTUGUERO Desayuno en el hotel y salida hacia Costa Rica, pasando por el Parque Nacional Braulio Carrillo para llegar hasta Matina, donde un bote nos lleva hasta Tortuguero. Llegada y alojamiento en el Hotel. Estancia en regimen de pensión completa.

9 TORTUGUERO Pensión completa. Día completo para explorar el maravilloso Parque Nacional de Tortuguero. Alojamiento.

10 TORTUGUERO - SAN JOSE. Desayuno en el lodge. Salida hacia San José. Almuerzo en ruta. Llegada por la tarde y traslado al hotel. Alojamiento.

11 SAN JOSE - ARENAL. Desayuno. Traslado a la zona del Volcán. Llegada y alojamiento.

12 ARENAL Desayuno. Día libre para disfrutar de esta zona norte. Alojamiento.

13 ARENAL - SAN JOSE Desayuno en el hotel y tralado a San José. Alojamiento.

14 SAN JOSE Desayuno. Excursión al Volcán Poas y Sarchi. Visita a las plantaciones de café, finas florales. Paseo por el bosque donde vamos a ver aves exóticas. Almuerzo incluido. Por la tarde traslado al hotel. Alojamiento.

15 SAN JOSE - ESPAÑA Desayuno en el hotel y traslado al aeropuerto. Noche a bordo.

16 ESPAÑA Llegada y fin de servicios.

G Haz una lista de resoluciones para el año próximo y coméntalas con tu compañero/a.

Ejemplo: Mi novio y yo vamos a dejar de fumar.

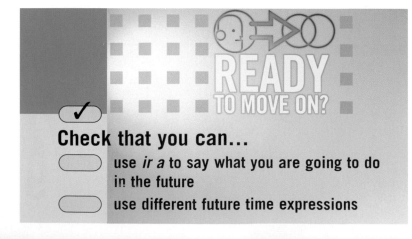

READY TO MOVE ON?

Check that you can...

- use *ir a* to say what you are going to do in the future
- use different future time expressions

Vacaciones en América Latina

AOL - [Costa Rica, Sin Ingredientes Artificiales]

File Edit Window Sign Off Help

▼EMAIL   ▼PEOPLE   ▼SERVICES   ▼CUSTOMISE   ▼INTERNET   ▼PLACES

Read | Write | I.M. | Chat | Parental Controls | My AOL | Web | Favourites | Shopping | Your Money

Hide Channels | ◁ | ▷ | http://www.visitcostarica.com/ict/paginas/ictnota.asp?idnota=51

COSTA RICA
Sin Ingredientes Artificiales

Centroamérica

| Cómo llegar | Información | Qué hacer | Adónde ir | Alojamiento | Desplazarse |

Poas Volcano - Central Valley

News

Reservaciones online

vuelos hoteles autos tours

Buscar

[   ] ir

Menú Principal
Inicio
Calendario de eventos
Mapas de Costa Rica
Galería de fotos
Novedades & Artículos
Cert. Sost. Turística (CST)
Instituto Turístico (ICT)
Folletos
Comunidad de Empresas Turísticas
Contáctenos

Historia

Herencia y cultura

La cultura costarricense es el reflejo de la mezcla de razas que coexisten en el país. La influencia principal es la europea, que se demuestra en aspectos como el idioma oficial -el español-, la arquitectura de las iglesias y otros edificios históricos. La influencia indígena es menos visible, pero está presente en las tortillas que son parte de la comida típica costarricense y las artesanías en cerámica que se vende a la orilla de las carreteras.

Una influencia más reciente es la que viene de Estados Unidos, que se percibe en muchas áreas desde las carteleras de cine en San José a las cadenas de comida rápida que abundan en sus ciudades. Un aspecto importante de la herencia cultural costarricense es su amor por la paz y la democracia. Los ticos tratan de destacar que su nación es la excepción de América Latina, ya que desde hace mucho tiempo la política es dominada por el sistema democrático y no por dictadores.

Los ticos se enorgullecen de tener más de un siglo de tradición democrática y más de 50 años sin ejército. Éste fue abolido en 1948, y el dinero que ahorra el país al no tener fuerzas armadas lo invierte en mejorar el nivel de vida de los costarricenses, lo que ayuda para la paz social, que hace de Costa Rica un lugar agradable para visitar.

El Tico

Los 'ticos', como también son conocidos los costarricenses, son famosos por ser gente hospitalaria y les gusta conservar esa reputación. Son educados y trabajadores, les gusta regalar una sonrisa a la gente y estrechar la mano.

Los ticos saben que su tierra es especial, y generalmente aceptan gustosos guiar a los visitantes que están perdidos, a veces incluso explicándoles cosas que pueden resultar extrañar para un extranjero, y hacen su estadía lo más placentera posible. Se dice que los ticos son el mejor activo de esta nación, y una vez que usted haya vivido su amistosidad y espontaneidad, ya no le quedará duda al respecto.

start | AOL - [Costa Rica, Si...   13:43

La rutina diaria

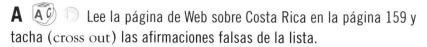

A  Lee la página de Web sobre Costa Rica en la página 159 y tacha (cross out) las afirmaciones falsas de la lista.

1 Tico es el nombre con el que se conoce a la gente de Costa Rica.

2 Su idioma oficial es el español.

3 Su población es el producto de una mezcla de razas europeas e indígenas, predominando las indígenas.

4 Su arquitectura y lengua son consecuencia de la influencia de la población indígena.

5 La población indígena también ha influido en la gastronomía.

6 La influencia estadounidense se puede apreciar en todos sitios.

7 Los costarriquenses están orgullosos de su sistema democrático.

8 Su tradición democrática es corta pero segura.

9 Su ejército desapareció hace medio siglo más o menos. La eliminación de este gasto ayuda su economía.

10 Hoy día el nivel de vida en Costa Rica es el más alto de América central.

B Investiga más en la página de Web y descubre:

1 ¿Cuál es la situación sanitaria?

2 ¿Qué índice de analfabetismo hay hoy día en Costa Rica?

3 ¿Existe la pena de muerte?

4 ¿Quién es Óscar Arias?

C ¿Qué crees que hace de Costa Rica un lugar agradable para visitar?

D Haz una lista de las atracciones turísticas que hayas descubierto.

E Escribe una carta a un(a) amigo/a hablándole sobre Costa Rica y recomendándole sitios para visitar, platos típicos para probar y cosas para hacer.

GLOSSARY

Nouns

alojamiento (m)	accommodation
aparcamiento (m)	car park
apartamento (m)	apartment, flat
camping (m)	campsite
cine (m)	cinema
clase (f)	class
conciorto (m)	concert
correspondencia (f)	correspondence
costumbre (f)	custom
deporte (m)	sport
despacho (m)	office
examen (m)	exam
excurslón (f)	excursion
exposición (f)	exhibition
fin de semana (m)	weekend
fútbol (m)	football
gimnasio (m)	gym
guía (m/f)	guide
hamaca (f)	deckchair
itinerario (m)	itinerary
jardín (m)	garden
matemáticas (fpl)	maths
mercado (m)	market
mito (m)	myth, legend
música (clásica) (f)	(classical) music
nota (f)	note
patio (m)	patio
película (f)	film
piso (m)	flat
regalo (m)	present

reserva (f)	reservation, booking
reunión (f)	meeting
sierra (f)	mountain range
siesta (f)	nap
tenis (m)	tennis
terraza (f)	terrace
traslado (m)	transfer
universidad (f)	university
vacaciones (fpl)	holiday
viaje (m)	journey
visita (f)	visit

Adjectives

bionvonido/a	welcome
increíble	incredible, unbelievable
ordenado/a	organized

Verbs

acostarse	to go to bed
arreglarse	to get ready
clasificar	to organise, sort
consultar	to consult
contestar	to answer
desayunar	to have breakfast
descansar	to rest
dormirse	to fall asleep
ducharse	to have a shower
echar cabezadas	to have a snooze, nod off
echarse la siesta	to take a nap
empezar	to start
encontrar	to meet, find

La rutina diaria

GLOSSARY

escuchar	to listen (to)
esquiar	to ski, go skiing
estudiar	to study
incluir	to include
ir de copas	to go for a drink
ir de vacaciones	to go on holiday
ir de vinos	to go for a drink
jugar	to play
lavarse	to wash (oneself)
levantarse	to get up
llamar por teléfono	to phone
nadar	to swim
organizar	to organize
parecer	to seem, appear
planear	to plan
preparar	to prepare
quedar	to stay
quedar con alguien	to arrange to meet someone
realizar	to do, carry out
romper	to break
soler	to be in the habit of, usually do
terminar	to finish
tomar el aperitivo	to have an aperitif/drink
tomar el sol	to sunbathe
ver	to see
vestirse	to get dressed
volver (a)	to go back, return

Time expressions

a menudo	often
a veces	sometimes
antes	before
casi siempre	almost always
de vez en cuando	from time to time
después	after
el año próximo	next year
el año que viene	next year
el mes próximo	next month
el mes que viene	next month
en primer lugar	firstly
finalmente	finally
la semana próxima	next week
la semana que viene	next week
luego	then
normalmente	normally
nunca	never
pasado mañana	the day after tomorrow
por lo general	usually, in general
seguidamente	then, next
siempre	always
sobre (las ocho)	about, around (eight o'clock)
tarde	late
temprano	early
una vez	once
dos/tres veces	twice / three times

Expressions

con vista al mar	with a sea view
Cuesta creer.	It's hard to believe.
Vamos a hablar.	Let's talk.
¡Vamos a ver!	Let's see. / We'll see.
se alquila	to let
se compra	wanted (to buy)
se vende	for sale

LOOKING FORWARD

In **Unit 10,** we will talk about what you like to do in your spare time, future plans and holidays you have been on. To prepare, look at these pictures.

| nadar | montar en bicicleta | escalar | bucear | jugar al tenis |

| esquiar | ir de excursión | tomar el sol | patinar | montar a caballo |

UNIT 10
Las vacaciones y el tiempo libre

UNIT **9**

UNIT 10
Las vacaciones
y el tiempo libre

By the end of this unit you will be able to:

- Say what you are going to do and what you did yesterday
- Talk about your holiday, saying where you went last year and what you did
- Say what you like to do in your spare time
- Say what you think of a place

1 ¿Qué recuerdas?

A Tres amigos (Ramón, Juan y Manuel) van a compartir (share) un piso. Deciden crear unas reglas (rules) para evitar problemas. Escucha y contesta las preguntas.

1 ¿Quién se levanta el primero?

2 ¿Quién se acuesta el último?

3 ¿Quiénes se duchan por las mañanas?

4 ¿Quiénes son estudiantes?

5 ¿Cuál de ellos prefiere el silencio por la tarde para estudiar?

B 🎲 ⭕ Lee las siguientes reglas y marca las que creas que son necesarias para que exista una buena convivencia entre Ramón, Juan y Manuel.

1 No poner la radio o música por las mañanas.

2 Bañarse sólo por la mañana.

3 Traer (Bring) amigos sólo por las tardes.

4 No hacer ruido (noise) después de las doce de la noche.

5 Comer fuera.

C 🗣️ ⭕ ¿Crees que son compatibles? ¿Quiénes crees que son más compatibles? y ¿por qué?

D 🎲 ⭕ Ordena estas palabras, conjuga los verbos en presente y añádele la preposición **a**, **en**, **de**, **por** o **para** si es necesario.

1 cenar sábados fuera todos los (nosotros)

2 discoteca la ir a veces (nosotros)

3 Laura y Yolanda deporte mucho hacer fines los semana

4 gustar caballo me montar

5 salir mañanas casa las temprano (yo)

6 tomar los todos la sol el playa veranos (nosotros)

7 paseo su ir Maruja y Ramón con perro

8 Carmina el tocar ahora piano

E 🗣️ ⭕ Haz una lista de cosas que crees que pueden pasar este año. Luego pon la lista en común con tus compañeros, haced una lista juntos y comprobar en cuántas coincidís.

Las vacaciones y el tiempo libre **10**

2 Fui a Madrid

A 🔤 🎧 📀 Lee la postal de Sebastián y subraya todos los verbos en pasado que aparecen. Luego haz una lista con todos los verbos y escribe el infinitivo.

12 de octubre

Querida Mariana:

¿Cómo estás? Como ves, estoy en Madrid. Llegué anteayer por la mañana. Después de comer visité el Palacio Real y compré esta postal. Por la tarde di un paseo por el Parque del Retiro. Ayer por la mañana me levanté temprano y fui al Paseo de la Castellana. Visité el museo del Prado y el Centro de Arte Reina Sofía, luego comí cerca de la estación de Atocha, pero no pude visitar el museo Thyssen-Bornemisza porque lo cerraron por reforma, por eso voy a ir pasado mañana. Por la tarde salí con unos amigos que viven en Madrid desde hace años. Fuimos a tomar unas cañas en la Cava Baja y luego fuimos a cenar. Cenamos en un restaurante muy bueno, cerca de la Plaza Mayor. Después de cenar nos fuimos de copas por la calle Huertas que es una zona de mucha marcha. Hoy me encuentro fatal. Creo que me voy a quedar todo el día en la cama, porque mañana voy a ir a Navacerrada a esquiar con mis amigos y necesito descansar. Escríbeme pronto.

Un abrazo

Sebastián

LEARNING TIP:
Marcha

Tiene mucha marcha.
He likes a good time
Hay mucha marcha.
There is a lot going on.

The simple past tense

When talking about completed events in the past, you use a different form of the verb. This form is called the simple past or preterite.

As usual, the verb endings change, depending on the subject. The simple past has two sets of endings, one for **–ar** verbs and another for **–er** and **–ir** verbs.

	–ar	**–er / –ir**	
	cenar	**comer**	**vivir**
yo	cen**é**	com**í**	viv**í**
tú	cen**aste**	com**iste**	viv**iste**
usted/él/ella	cen**ó**	com**ió**	viv**ió**
nosotros/as	cen**amos**	com**imos**	viv**imos**
vosotros/as	cen**asteis**	com**isteis**	viv**isteis**
ustedes/ellos/ellas	cen**aron**	com**ierion**	viv**ieron**

Anoche cené en mi restaurante favorito.

Last night I had dinner in my favourite restaurant.

Comieron con sus abuelos.

They had lunch with their grandparents.

¿Viviste en Madrid el año pasado?

Did you live in Madrid last year?

No comimos fruta ayer.

We didn't eat any fruit yesterday.

LEARNING TIP:
Past vs present

For regular **–ar** and **–ir** verbs (not **–er** verbs or irregular verbs), you will note that the **nosotros** form of the verb is the same in the present simple and in the past simple. You can usually tell from the context which is meant.

LEARNING TIP:

When talking about the future or the past, specific words are often used, e.g. **ayer**, **mañana**, **el año pasado**.

pasado	last
próximo / que viene	next

B Estudia el vocabulario siguiente y ponlo en orden cronológico. Luego escribe un ejemplo, diciendo qué hiciste tú en esos momentos.

> mañana   anteayer   el mes pasado
> el año próximo   anoche   el año pasado
> el mes que viene   ayer   en Navidad
> el otro día   la semana pasada   hace unos días

C Rellena los huecos con el pasado del verbo en paréntesis. Cuidado con el sujeto.

1   Ayer mi padre y yo ⬭ (comer) en casa de mi abuela.

2   La semana pasada Juan ⬭ (jugar) al baloncesto (basketball) con mi equipo.

3   Anteayer mis amigos ⬭ (correr) la maratón.

4   Creo que anoche tú ⬭ (beber) demasiado.

5   El fin de semana pasado mi compañero y yo ⬭ (estudiar) juntos para el examen de hoy.

6   ¿ ⬭ (ver) esta película el domingo?

7   Ayer toda mi familia ⬭ (cenar) junta.

8   El año pasado ⬭ (vivir) en Francia.

9   Julio Iglesias no ⬭ (ganar) el festival de Eurovisión.

10 Mis amigos ⬭ (escuchar) el concierto de Christina Aguilera desde fuera.

D Escribe un correo electrónico a un amigo y cuéntale qué hiciste ayer. Contesta estas preguntas:

- ¿A qué hora te levantaste? • ¿Qué desayunaste? • ¿Dónde comiste? •
¿Trabajaste? • ¿Estudiaste? • ¿Viste a tus amigos? etc.

| ¡Hola! |
| Ayer fue un día magnífico … |

E Mariana no recibió la carta de Sebastián (actividad 2A). Escucha las cinco preguntas de Mariana a Sebastián sobre lo que hizo durante las vacaciones y contéstalas.

Check that you can...
- say what you did and where you went yesterday
- speak about past events

3 ¿*Ser* o *ir*?

LANGUAGE FOCUS

The past simple forms of **ir** and **ser** are irregular and identical; the context will clarify which verb is meant.

Ayer **fue** a una fiesta, **fue** una fiesta muy divertida.

Yesterday he went to a party. It was a very lively party.

ser (to be) and **ir** (to go)

yo	**fui**	*I was, I went*
tú	**fuiste**	*you were, you went*
usted	**fue**	*you were, you went*
él/ella	**fue**	*he/she was, he/she went*
nosotros/as	**fuimos**	*we were, we went*
vosotros/as	**fuisteis**	*you were, you went*
ustedes	**fueron**	*you were, you went*
ellos/ellas	**fueron**	*they were, they went*

A Rellena los huecos con los verbos **ir** y **ser**.

1 Mis padres *fueron* a la fiesta de Juan.

2 Yo ( ) el primero en llegar a la fiesta.

3 Raquel y Alejandro ( ) los protagonistas de la fiesta.

4 Tú ( ) demasiado amable con los invitados.

5 Alberto ( ) muy generoso con su regalo.

6 Mi hermana y yo ( ) a bailar después de la fiesta.

7 Y vosotros no ( ) a la discoteca.

B Ahora traduce las frases anteriores.

4 Aún hay más números

LANGUAGE FOCUS

Here are some examples of how to form numbers over 999:

1.000	mil
2.000	dos mil
39.000	treinta y nueve mil
548.000	quinientos cuarenta y ocho mil
1.000.000	un millón

Mil is used for dates, when said in full.
Cristóbal Colón descubrió América en **mil cuatrocientos noventa y dos**.
Christopher Columbus discovered America in 1492.

En **mil novecientos sesenta y nueve** el hombre aterrizó en la luna.
In 1969, man landed on the Moon.

Remember that in Spain and other European countries, thousands are divided with a dot:
3.976€ tres mil novecientos setenta y seis euros

Commas are used for decimals:
3,97€ tres euros con noventa y siete céntimos

A Escribe estos números con letra.

1	16 *dieciséis*	**5**	519.316
2	316	**6**	1.519.316
3	9.316	**7**	12.519.316
4	19.316		

B Completa según el modelo.

1 tres mil quinientos cuarenta y seis 3.546 ⊠⊠ 6.453 seis mil cuatrocientos cincuenta y tres

2 (_____) 9.267 ⊠⊠ (_____) siete mil seiscientos veintinueve

3 (_____) 12.381 ⊠⊠ (_____) (_____)

➜

Las vacaciones y el tiempo libre UNIT

4 (   ) (   ) ⊠⊠ 57.329 (   )

5 (   ) 683.542⊠⊠ (   ) (   )

6 (   ) (   ) ⊠⊠ 854.361 (   )

7 (   ) 23.456.851⊠⊠ 15.865.432 (   )

C Lee en alto estas frases con sus cifras.

1 La población en Guinea Ecuatorial es de unos 390.000 habitantes.

2 La superficie es de 28.050km^2.

3 España tiene una extensión de 504.750km^2.

4 El Teide es la montaña más alta de España con 3.710m.

5 En 1616 murieron Cervantes y Shakespeare.

6 El salario mínimo español en el año 2003 fue de 6.316,80€.

5 *Estar* y *tener*

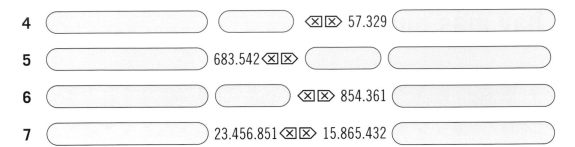

LANGUAGE FOCUS

Estar and **tener** are very similar in the past simple. Notice that the endings have no written accent, unlike regular past simple verbs.

	estar = to be	**tener** = to have			
yo	es**tuve**	**tuve**	nosotros/as	es**tuvimos**	**tuvimos**
tú	es**tuviste**	**tuviste**	vosotros/as	es**tuvisteis**	**tuvisteis**
usted	es**tuvo**	**tuvo**	ustedes	es**tuvieron**	**tuvieron**
él/ella	es**tuvo**	**tuvo**	ellos/ellas	es**tuvieron**	**tuvieron**

A 🎲 ✏️ 🎧 💿 Rellena los huecos de esta carta con el pasado de uno de estos verbos.

(**ser   estar   ir   tener**)

Querida Barbara:

Estoy en Valencia de vacaciones. Anteayer (1) _____ en Benijófar, un pueblecito de la costa. (2) _____ con unos amigos y ayer (3) _____ en Orihuela y Torrevieja. En Orihuela (4) _____ a visitar la casa-museo de Miguel Hernández, allí (5) _____ toda la mañana. Por la tarde (6) _____ a la playa y (7) _____ tomando el sol toda la tarde. Por la noche, antes de volver a Valencia, (8) _____ a casa de tu primo Borja para saludarlo. Se alegró mucho de verme y (9) _____ muy amable con nosotros – nos invitó a cenar en un restaurante típico de la zona. La ccna (10) _____ buenísima, lo pasamos muy bien. En general (11) _____ unos días muy tranquilos y agradables. Anoche Luis y yo (12) _____ que alquilar un taxi para volver a Valencia, porque Carlos (13) _____ que volver a Valencia antes de cenar.

Ahora tengo que dejarte.
Escríbeme pronto, besos

Jacobo

B 🎧 💿 Escucha a Juanma hablar sobre el fin de semana pasado y marca lo que coincida con la agenda. Luego cambia los verbos al pasado.

VIERNES	DOMINGO
Examen de historia 10:00	Ir a montar a caballo
Comprar regalo para Paloma	Parque a las 5:00
SÁBADO	Preparar las vacaciones de esquí
Piscina municipal	
Comer en casa	
Pista de patinaje	
Disco	

C 🗣️ 🎲 🎧 💿 Juega con tu compañero/a a las "Tres en raya" (noughts and crosses). Cada uno elige una de estas expresiones y forma una frase; si la frase es correcta la casilla es suya. El primero en conseguir tres casillas en línea gana.

ayer	el próximo año	la semana pasada
pasado mañana	anteanoche	mañana
anoche	el mes que viene	hoy

10

D Lee estas frases, y escribe el verbo en el pasado. Luego haz la pregunta correspondiente a cada frase.

(yo comer) fuera con Juan → Comí fuera con Juan.

¿Dónde comiste? / ¿Con quién comiste?

1 (ellos levantarse) muy temprano

2 (ella ir) a correr al parque

3 (él desayunar) en el club de tenis

4 (Juan, Carlos, Maite y yo jugar) un partido de dobles

5 (yo ir) con el perro a pasear

6 No, (Maite ir) de compras conmigo

7 (yo tener) que estudiar mucho para el examen

E Escucha la historia y contesta las preguntas.

1 ¿Se levantó temprano Juanjo ayer?

2 ¿Por qué no desayunó?

3 ¿Por qué tomó un taxi?

4 ¿A quién vio en la oficina?

5 ¿Por qué no había gente en la oficina?

READY TO MOVE ON?

✓

Check that you can...

- say what you did yesterday using irregular verbs
- talk about holidays you have had, saying where you went and what you did.
- speak about past events using irregular verbs

6 Gente importante

A  Lee los puntos relevantes de la vida de "Evita" y escribe su biografía, cambiando el presente por el pretérito.

Una argentina ilustre, ¡una líder espiritual!

Eva Duarte de Perón (Evita)

❖ Nace el 7 de mayo de 1919 en Los Toldos (Provincia de Buenos Aires).

❖ Hija ilegítima de Juan Duarte y Juana Ibarguren (una cocinera).

❖ Cantante y actriz radiofónica.

❖ En 1944 conoce al general Perón en una obra benéfica (*para ayudar a las víctimas del terremoto ocurrido en la provincia de San Juan*).

❖ En 1945 Perón es detenido y Evita moviliza a los sindicatos para liberarlo.

❖ Una vez libre, se casa con él en la ciudad de La Plata.

❖ Ese año y el siguiente participa en la campaña presidencial de su marido.

❖ Enseguida se gana la adulación de las masas, a los que ella llama "descamisados".

❖ Un año más tarde Perón accede a la presidencia y ella se convierte en una poderosa líder a su lado.

❖ A pesar de no tener un puesto oficial en el gobierno, Evita actúa como Ministro de Salud y Trabajo.

❖ Crea la Fundación Eva Perón (la sostiene con "voluntarios" y contribuciones, más aportes de la lotería nacional y otros fondos).

❖ La fundación establece cientos de hospitales, escuelas, orfanatos, casas para personas de edad y otras instituciones de caridad.

❖ Tiene muchos enemigos en la élite tradicional.

❖ En 1947, a sus 28 años, viaja a Europa enviada por Perón como una embajadora no oficial ante el nuevo mundo de la posguerra. Visita España, Francia, Italia y Suiza. Es agasajada por los Jefes de Estado y por el propio Papa Pío XII.

❖ Evita es responsable del voto femenino y forma el Partido Feminista Peronista en 1949.

❖ También introduce la educación religiosa obligatoria en todas las escuelas argentinas.

❖ En 1951, a pesar de padecer de cáncer, es nominada para la vicepresidencia, pero el ejército la obliga a renunciar a tal candidatura.

❖ Muere el 26 de julio de 1952.

❖ Aunque su vida es corta, impulsa toda una serie de transformaciones sociales.

B Piensa en la vida de alguna celebridad. Imagina que tú eres esta persona y escribe un pequeño resumen sobre tu vida, sin mencionar tu nombre. Luego lee tu "biografía" en alto para tus compañeros y contesta sus preguntas.

Puedes utilizar estos verbos para ayudarte:

> casarse   nacer   tener un/dos hijo(s)   empezar
> terminar   volver   conseguir   ir   divorciarse
> conocer   volver a casarse

C Escucha a tu compañero/a contar "su" vida, y hazle preguntas para averiguar quién es.

- ¿Qué cuadros pintaste?
- ¿Qué libros escribiste?
- ¿Cuál es/fue tu obra más conocida?
- ¿Dónde naciste?
- ¿En qué año naciste?

D Usa toda la información que tienes y escribe tu propia biografía. Termínala contando tus planes para el futuro.

READY
TO MOVE ON?

✔

Check that you can...

- ask questions and reply using the past simple
- talk about the lives of famous people
- speak and write about what you have done in the past and what are you going to do in the future

7 Pasado y futuro

A ✍ 🔊 Escribe una carta a tu mejor amigo/a. Dile adónde fuiste de vacaciones el año pasado y lo que hiciste. No olvides decirle:

- tu opinión del lugar
- si te gustó o no, y por qué
- lo que te gusta hacer cuando estás de vacaciones
- adónde vas a ir de vacaciones el año que viene y lo que vas a hacer

B 🔊 👥 🔊 Con tu compañero/a habla sobre qué lugares te gustan para tus vacaciones y por qué, qué te gusta hacer cuando estás de vacaciones y adónde vas a ir la próxima vez. No olvides mencionar cosas que vayas a hacer.

Podéis ayudaros con estas preguntas:

- ¿A dónde fuiste de vacaciones la última vez?
- ¿Te gustó? ¿Por qué (no)?
- ¿Qué es lo que más te gustó?, ¿y lo que menos?
- ¿Cómo es …?
- ¿Adónde vas a ir la próxima vez? ¿Con quién? ¿Qué vas a hacer?

Descubre el mundo HISPANO

Argentina y unos argentinos ilustres

A ¿Cuánto sabes sobre Argentina? En grupos tratad de contestar estas preguntas.

1 ¿Cuál es el baile nacional argentino?

2 ¿Qué es la Pampa?

3 ¿Cuál es la capital de Argentina?

4 ¿Qué es un gaucho?

5 ¿Quién es el actual presidente de Argentina?

6 ¿Dónde está la Tierra del Fuego?

7 ¿Qué es el mate?

8 ¿Cuál es el producto más exportado de la Argentina?

B En parejas tratad de unir estos argentinos famosos con su definición.

1 Carlos Gardel   **a** Poderosa líder argentina.

2 Guillermo Vilas   **b** Le puso voz al tango.

3 Eva Perón   **c** El mejor tenista argentino de todos los tiempos.

4 Gabriel Batistuta   **d** Escribió poemas, cuentos … Escritor muy polémico.

5 Jorge Luis Borges   **e** El fenomenal goleador argentino.

GLOSSARY

Nouns

baloncesto (m)	basketball
deberes (mpl)	homework
discoteca (f)	disco, club
equipo (m)	team
esquí (m)	skiing
fiesta (f)	party
gente (f)	people
historia (f)	history, story
invitado/a (m/f)	guest
maratón (f)	marathon
Navidad (f)	Christmas
piano (m)	piano
piscina municipal (f)	(council) swimming pool
pista de patinaje (f)	ice rink
posguerra (f)	postwar
radio (f)	radio
taxi (m)	taxi

Adjectives

amable	friendly
conocido/a	someone you know
demasiado/a	too (much/many)
divertido/a	funny, amusing
doble (habitación)	double (room)
ilustre	famous, illustrious
junto/a	together
siguiente	following

Verbs

alcanzar	to reach, attain
alejarse (de)	to distance oneself (from)
bailar	to dance
bucear	to scuba dive
casarse	to get married
colaborar (con)	to collaborate, work (with)
conseguir	to get, obtain
correr	to run
dar un paseo	to go for a walk

GLOSSARY

decidir	to decide
decir	to say
divorciarse	to get divorced
ganar	to win
inaugurar	to inaugurate
ir de excursión	to go on a trip
montar a caballo	to go horseriding
montar en bicicleta	to ride a bike
morir	to die
nacer	to be born
pasear	to walk, stroll
patinar	to skate
pedir	to ask for
poner	to put
saber	to know

tocar	to play (an instrument)
traer	to bring

Time expressions

anoche	last night
anteayer	the day before yesterday
ayer	yesterday
el año pasado	last year
el mes pasado	last month
hace unos días	a few days ago
la semana pasada	last week

Expressions

tener marcha	to be energetic

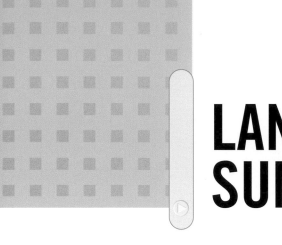

LANGUAGE SUMMARY

Nouns

Spanish has two genders. Nouns are either masculine or feminine:

mesa   *table* (feminine)
libro   *book* (masculine)

In general, if a noun ends in **o**, it is masculine, and if it ends in **a**, it is feminine.

General rules for forming the plural:
- ending in a vowel: add an **–s**
  primos   *cousins*
- ending in a consonant, add **–es**
  españoles   *Spanish people*

Articles

The definite article

The article *the* is translated into Spanish by **el**, **la**, **los** or **las**, depending on whether the noun is masculine or feminine, singular or plural.

el pollo (*the chicken*)   masculine singular
la naranja (*the orange*)   feminine singular

los guisantes (*the peas*)   masculine plural
las verduras (*the vegetables*)   feminine plural

The indefinite article

un pollo (*a chicken*)   masculine singular
una naranja (*an orange*)   feminine singular
unos guisantes (*some peas*)   masculine plural
unas verduras (*some vegetables*) feminine plural

In Spanish, the words for *a* or *an* are not used when talking about jobs or occupations.
Soy professor.   *I'm a teacher*.

Adjectives

Spanish adjectives agree in gender and number with the nouns they describe. The form you see in the dictionary is usually the masculine singular form.

To make the feminine form, you need to change the adjective:

1 Adjectives ending in **–o** change to **–a**:
  chin**o** → chin**a**
2 Adjectives ending in **–e** or **–u** do not change:
  estadounidense → estadounidense
3 Most adjectives ending in a consonant add **–a**:
  español → español**a**

Adjectives (including nationalities) that have an accent on the last syllable lose the accent in the feminine form:
japonés → japonesa   inglés → inglesa

Comparatives

There are three main ways of comparing things in Spanish.

1 Equality (*as ... as ...*)

If the comparison is based on an adjective, the expression to use is:

tan + adjective + **como**

Alaska es **tan** fría **como** la Tierra del Fuego.   *Alaska is as cold as Tierra del Fuego.*

If the comparison is based on a noun, use:

tanto/a/os/as + noun + **como**

En Buenos Aires hay **tantos** teatros **como** en Nueva York.   *In Buenos Aires, there are as many theatres as in New York.*

2 Superiority (*bigger/more ... than*)

Use:

más + adjective/noun + **que**

Perú es **más** grande **que** Ecuador.   *Peru is bigger than Ecuador.*

Chile tiene **más** costa **que** Ecuador.   *Chile has more coastline than Ecuador.*

3 Inferiority (*smaller/less ... than*)

Use:

menos + adjective/noun + **que**

Ecuador es **menos** grande **que** Perú.   *Ecuador is smaller than Peru.*

Ecuador tiene **menos** costa **que** Chile.   *Ecuador has less coastline than Chile.*

Possessive adjectives

mi	*my*	**mi** libro = *my book*	
mis	*my*	**mis** libros = *my books*	
tu	*your*	**tu** libro = *your* (sing.) *book*	
tus	*your*	**tus** libros = *your* (sing.) *books*	
su	*his/her/its*	**su** libro = *his/her book / your book* (usted)	
sus	*his/her/its*	**sus** libros = *his/her books / your books* (usted)	
nuestro/a	*our*	**nuestro** libro = *our book*	
nuestros/as	*our*	**nuestros** libros = *our books*	
vuestro/a	*your* (pl.)	**vuestro** libro = *your* (pl.)*book*	
vuestros/as	*your* (pl.)	**vuestros** libros = *your* (pl.) *books*	
su	*their/your* (pl.) formal	**su** libro = *their/your book* (ustedes)	
sus	*their/your* (pl.) formal	**sus** libros = *their/your books* (ustedes)	

Possessive adjectives have to match the number and gender of the nouns they describe:

Nuestro hijo es muy alto pero **nuestra** hija no es alta.   *Our son is very tall, but our daughter is not tall.*

Vuestros zapatos son blancos y **vuestras** chaquetas son negras.   *Your shoes are white and your jackets are black.*

Demonstrative adjectives and pronouns

Demonstrative adjectives (*this/that/these/those*) agree in number as well as gender with the thing they refer to.

	Masculine	Feminine	
Singular	éste	ésta	*this (one)*
Plural	éstos	éstas	*these (ones)*

Quisiera vino tinto.   *I would like some red wine.*
– ¿Quiere **éste**?   *– Would you like this one?*

The words for *that (one)* and *those (ones)* work in a similar way.

	Masculine	Feminine	
Singular	ése	ésa	*that*
Plural	ésos	ésas	*those*

	Masculine	Feminine	
Singular	aquél	aquélla	*that (further away)*
Plural	aquéllos	aquéllas	*those (further away)*

Spanish has two words for *that*: **ese** and **aquel**. **Aquel** is used to describe things that are further away from the speaker than **ese**.

Quisiera una manzana.   *I'd like an apple.*
–¿**Ésa**?   *–That one?*
No, **aquélla**.   *No, that one (over there).*

When **este**, **ese**, **aquel** are used with the noun (as adjectives), they don't have an accent. When they replace the noun (as pronouns), they have the accent. The accent doesn't affect the way you say the word.

Prepositions

Spanish prepositions can have different meanings from English ones. Some of the most important prepositions are:

a
This common preposition has various meanings:
- *to* when referring to a destination:
  Quiero ir **a** la estación, por favor.   *I want to go to the station, please.*
- *at* when telling the time:
  a las seis y media   *at half past six*
- *away* when used with a distance:
  Está **a** seis kilómetros.   *It's six kilometres away.*

de

Another common preposition, it can be used:
- to mean *from* when referring to origins:
  Juan es **de** Barcelona.   *Juan is from Barcelona.*
- to mean *of* referring to content:
  un bocadillo **de** chorizo   *a chorizo sandwich*
- to indicate possession:
  El coche es **de** Carmina.   *The car is Carmina's.*
- to show what something is made of:
  unos guantes **de** piel   *some leather gloves*
- in expressions of time:
  de la tarde, **de** la mañana   *in the afternoon/morning*

hasta

This means *until* or *as far as*, either in place or time, with a sense of end:
Todo recto **hasta** el final de la calle.
Straight ahead as far as the end of the street.
hasta las cinco   *until five o'clock*

en

Be careful with this one, as it doesn't always translate as *in*:
El coche está **en** la plaza.   *The car is in the square.*
Mi bolso está **en** el coche.   *My bag is in the car.*
El libro está **en** la mesa.   *The book is on the table.*

para

This has different meanings and can sometimes be confusing, but it generally means *for* or *in the direction of*:
Los calamares **para** mí.   *The squid for me.*
El vuelo IB381 sale **para** Bilbao.
Flight IB381 is leaving for Bilbao.

por

Like **para**, **por** has many meanings; the most common are *through* and *along*.
El tren de Sevilla pasa **por** Córdoba.
The Seville train goes through Cordoba.
Sigue recto **por** esta calle.
Go straight ahead along this street.

It is also used in many expressions:
por la mañana/tarde   *in the morning/evening*
por favor   *please*

desde

This means *from* or *since*:
desde aquí   *from here*
desde las dos   *since two o'clock*

Remember the contractions when followed by a noun:
a + el = al
de + el = del

Voy **al** supermercado.   *I'm going to the supermarket.*
Está delante **del** cine.   *It's in front of the cinema.*

Personal pronouns

yo	*I*
tú	*you* (informal)
usted	*you* (formal)
él	*he*
ella	*she*
nosotros/nosotras	*we*
vosotros/vosotras	*you* (pl. informal)
ustedes	*you* (pl. formal)
ellos/ellas	*they*

Tú is used with people you know, or people of your own age and in informal situations.

Usted is used with older people or in more formal situations.

Spanish speakers use **tutéame** when they want to be informal. It means *Please use the **tú** form with me.*

In Spanish, the personal pronouns are often omitted, as the verb will show you who is carrying out the action:
¿De dónde eres? – Soy española.
¿Dónde vives? – Vivo en Madrid.

Occasionally the personal pronouns are used for clarity or emphasis:
Yo soy de Madrid. *I'm from Madrid.*

Verbs: present tense

Regular verbs

–ar verb:	**comprar**	(*to buy*)
yo	**compro**	*I buy*
tú	**compras**	*you buy* (informal)
usted	**compra**	*you buy* (formal)
él/ella	**compra**	*he/she buys*
nosotros/as	**compramos**	*we buy*
vosotros/as	**compráis**	*you buy* (informal pl.)
ustedes	**compran**	*you buy* (formal pl.)
ellos/ellas	**compran**	*they buy*

–er verb:	**vender**	(*to sell*)
yo	**vendo**	*I sell*
tú	**vendes**	*you sell* (informal)
usted	**vende**	*you sell* (formal)
él/ella	**vende**	*he/she sells*
nosotros/as	**vendemos**	*we sell*
vosotros/as	**vendéis**	*you sell* (informal pl.)
ustedes	**venden**	*you sell* (formal pl.)
ellos/ellas	**venden**	*they sell*

–ir verb:	**vivir**	(*to live*)
yo	**vivo**	*I live*
tú	**vives**	*you live* (informal)
usted	**vive**	*you live* (formal)
él	**vive**	*he lives*
ella	**vive**	*she lives*
nosotros/as	**vivimos**	*we live*
vosotros/as	**vivís**	*you live* (informal pl.)
ustedes	**viven**	*you live* (formal pl.)
ellos/ellas	**viven**	*they live*

Irregular verbs

Ser and estar

ser (*to be*)

yo	**soy**	*I am*
tú	**eres**	*you are*
usted	**es**	*you are*
él/ella	**es**	*he/she is*
nosotros/as	**somos**	*we are*
vosotros/as	**sois**	*you are*
ustedes	**son**	*you are*
ellos/ellas	**son**	*they are*

Ser and **estar** both mean *to be*, but are used in different ways.

estar (*to be*)

yo	**estoy**	*I am*
tú	**estás**	*you are*
usted	**está**	*you are*
él/ella	**está**	*he/she is*
nosotros/as	**estamos**	*we are*
vosotros/as	**estáis**	*you are*
ustedes	**están**	*you are*
ellos/ellas	**están**	*they are*

Ser is used for permanent situations, e.g. who you are, where you are from, what you are like, what you do for a living.
Ésta **es** Carmen. Carmen **es** mi amiga, **es** chilena. Ella **es** morena, alta, guapa y simpática. Carmen y yo **somos** estudiantes.

Estar is used for more temporary situations, e.g. how you are, if you are single or married, and also to say where a place is:

¿Cómo **estás**?   **Estoy** bien, gracias.
¿**Estás** casada?   No, **estoy** soltera.
¿Dónde **está** Carmen?   **Está** en el museo.

Other irregular verbs

There are a number of irregular verbs in Spanish. Some are irregular in the first person singular:

salir → **Salgo** a las ocho y media de la mañana.
hacer→ **Hago** los deberes todos los días.

Others change in the middle (the stem):

empezar (*to start*) → **Empiezo** a trabajar a las nueve de la mañana.

Some have both irregularities:

tener → Siempre **tengo** mucho trabajo porque el Sr. Doughty tiene demasiadas responsabilidades.

Here are some of the most common irregular verbs:

	tener	*to have*
(yo)	**tengo**	*I have*
(tú)	**tienes**	*you have* (informal)
(usted)	**tiene**	*you have* (formal)
(él)	**tiene**	*he has*
(ella)	**tiene**	*she has*
(nosotros/as)	**tenemos**	*we have*
(vosotros/as)	**tenéis**	*you have* (informal pl.)
(ustedes)	**tienen**	*you have* (formal pl.)
(ellos/ellas)	**tienen**	*they have*

ir – *to go*		
(yo)	**voy**	*I go*
(tú)	**vas**	*you go* (informal)
(usted)	**va**	*you go* (formal)
(él)	**va**	*he goes*
(ella)	**va**	*she goes*
(nosotros/as)	**vamos**	*we go*
(vosotros/as)	**vais**	*you go* (informal pl.)
(ustedes)	**van**	*you go* (formal pl.)
(ellos/ellas)	**van**	*they go*

poder – *to be able to (can)*

(yo)	**puedo**	*I can*
(tú)	**puedes**	*you can* (informal)
(usted)	**puede**	*you can* (formal)
(él/ella)	**puede**	*he/she can*
(nosotros/as)	**podemos**	*we can*
(vosotros/as)	**podéis**	*you can* (informal pl.)
(ustedes)	**pueden**	*you can* (formal pl.)
(ellos/ellas)	**pueden**	*they can*

Reflexive verbs

In the infinitive, these are shown by adding **se** to the end of the verb (**llamarse**, **lavantarse**, etc.) However, the reflexive pronoun changes, depending on the subject:

me **Me** llamo Eva.
I'm called Eva.

te ¿Cómo **te** llamas?
What are you called?

se **Se** levanta tarde.
He gets up late.

nos Nosotros **nos** levantamos muy temprano y **nos** vestimos.
We get up very early and get dressed.

os Vosotros **os** acostáis demasiado tarde y **os** dormís enseguida.
You go to bed too late and fall asleep at once.

se Ellos **se** levantan siempre los primeros y **se** visten los últimos.
They always get up first and get dressed last.

Verbs: simple past tense

When talking about completed events in the past, you use the simple past or preterite.

Regular verbs

The simple past has two sets of endings, one for **–ar** verbs and another for **–er** and **–ir** verbs.

	–ar	**–er / –ir**	
	cenar	**comer**	**vivir**
yo	cené	comí	viví
tú	cenaste	comiste	viviste
él/ella/usted	cenó	comió	vivió
nosotros/as	cenamos	comimos	vivimos
vosotros/as	cenasteis	comisteis	vivisteis
ellos/ellas/ustedes	cenaron	comierion	vivieron

Irregular verbs

Many common verbs are irregular in the past simple. You need to learn them:

hacer   hice, hiciste, hizo, hicimos, hicisteis, hicieron
decir   dije, dijiste, dijo, dijimos, dijisteis, dijeron
venir   vine, viniste, vino, vinimos, vinisteis, vinieron
ver   vi, viste, vio, vimos, visteis, vieron

Others have minor spelling changes in the first person singular:
llegar → **llegué**
jugar → **jugué**

The past simple forms of **ir** and **ser** are irregular and identical; the context will clarify which verb is referred to.
Ayer **fui** a una fiesta, **fue** una fiesta muy divertida.
Yesterday I went to a party. It was a very lively party.

ser (*to be*) and **ir** (*to go*)

yo	**fui**	*I was, I went*	nosotros/as	**fuimos**	*we were, we went*
tú	**fuiste**	*you were, you went*	vosotros/as	**fuisteis**	*you were, you went*
usted	**fue**	*you were, you went*	ustedes	**fueron**	*you were, you went*
él/ella	**fue**	*he/she was, he/she went*	ellos/ellas	**fueron**	*they were, they went*

Estar and **tener** are very similar in the past simple. Notice that the endings have no written accent, unlike regular past simple verbs.

	estar (*to be*)	tener (*to have*)			
yo	estuve	tuve	nosotros/as	estuvimos	tuvimos
tú	estuviste	tuviste	vosotros/as	estuvisteis	tuvisteis
usted	estuvo	tuvo	ustedes	estuvieron	tuvieron
él/ella	estuvo	tuvo	ellos/ellas	estuvieron	tuvieron

Future with *ir a*

Ir a + infinitive is used to express future plans or say what is going to happen:

yo	**voy**
tú	**vas**
usted/él/ella	**va**
nosotros/as	**vamos**
vosotros/as	**vais**
ustedes/ellos/ellas	**van**

a + infinitive

Mañana **voy a** jugar al fútbol. *Tomorrow I am going to play football*
En diciembre **van a** esquiar en los Pirineos. *In December they are going to ski in the Pyrenees.*

Imperative

The imperative is used for commands or instructions. There are different forms, depending on whether you are addressing the person as **usted** or **tú**.

	Formal (**usted**)	Informal (**tú**)
take	tome	toma
follow	siga	sigue
turn	tuerza / doble	tuerce / dobla
cross	cruce	cruza

Toma la primera a la derecha y **sigue** la calle hasta el final. *Take the first on the right and follow the street to the end.*

Object pronouns

	Masculine	Feminine	
Singular	**lo**	**la**	*it*
Plural	**los**	**las**	*them*

Object pronouns usually come before the verb:

Quisiera un abrigo. **Lo** quiero negro.
Quisiera unos pantalones. **Los** quiero azules.
Quisiera una camisa. **La** quiero blanca.
Quisiera unas botas. **Las** quiero verdes.

But if the verb is an infinitive or imperative, it is added onto the end of the verb:

– ¿Qué tal las botas? ¿**Las** compra? or ¿Va a comprar**las**?
– No sé.
– ¡Cómpre**las**! (*Buy them!*)

Expressing likes and dislikes

To express likes and dislikes, you use the verb **gustar**.

me gusta / me gustan	*I like*
te gusta / te gustan	*you like* (informal singular)
le gusta / le gustan	*he/she likes / you like* (formal singular)
nos gusta / nos gustan	*we like*
os gusta / os gustan	*you like* (informal plural)
les gusta / les gustan	*they like/you like* (formal plural)

Gustar literally means *to please* and the thing that is liked is the subject of the verb. So if that thing is singular, you use **gusta**; if it is plural, you use **gustan**. The pronoun before the verb indicates the person who does the liking.

Me gusta la paella.	*I like paella.*
Nos gusta el vino.	*We like wine.*

Me gustan los mariscos.	*I like seafood.*
Les gustan las espinacas.	*They like spinach.*

Gustar can also be followed by a verb, in which case you use **gusta**:

Me **gusta comer** paella.	*I like eating paella.*
Le **gusta beber** vino.	*He likes drinking wine.*

To express dislikes, just put **no** in front:

No me gusta el café.	*I don't like coffee.*
No le gustan las galletas.	*She doesn't like biscuits.*

When you love doing something, you say **Me encanta …** or **Me encantan … Encantar** follows the same rules as **gustar**, so the verb agrees with the thing you love.

Me encanta la música.	*I love music.*
Me encantan las películas españolas.	*I love Spanish films.*

Numbers

1	uno	8	ocho	15	quince	22	veintidós	50	cincuenta
2	dos	9	nueve	16	dieciséis	23	veintitrés	60	sesenta
3	tres	10	diez	17	diecisiete	30	treinta	70	setenta
4	cuatro	11	once	18	dieciocho	31	treinta y uno	80	ochenta
5	cinco	12	doce	19	diecinueve	32	treinta y dos	90	noventa
6	seis	13	trece	20	veinte	33	treinta y tres	100	cien
7	iete	14	catorce	21	veintiuno	40	cuarenta		

The numbers from 0 to 30 are written as one word, e.g. **veintitrés**.
From 31, the numbers are written separately with **y** (*and*), e.g. **setenta y seis**.
Note that you don't need to put **uno** in front of **cien**: **cien** = *one/a hundred*

101 to 199 are formed using the word **ciento**:

101	ciento uno
102	ciento dos
123	ciento veintitrés
145	ciento cuarenta y cinco

200 to 999 are formed using the suffix **cientos**:

200	doscientos
300	trescientos
400	cuatrocientos
500	quinientos
600	seiscientos
700	setecientos
800	ochocientos
900	novecientos

209	doscientos nueve
437	cuatrocientos treinta y siete
568	quinientos sesenta y ocho
715	setecientos quince
925	novecientos veinticinco

Be careful with **quinientos** (500), **setecientos** (700) and **novecientos** (900), which don't follow the normal pattern of adding **cientos** to the number.

For numbers over 999, see the Language Focus on page 171.

Time

- For times on the hour, use **Son/Es la(s) ... en punto.**
Es la una en punto.	1:00 / 13:00
Son las dos en punto.	2:00 / 14:00
Son las seis en punto.	6:00 / 18:00

- For half past the hour, use **Son/Es la(s) ... y media.**
Es la una y media.	1:30 / 13:30
Son las tres y media.	3:30 / 15:30
Son las siete y media.	7:30 / 19:30

- For quarter past the hour, use **Son/Es la(s) ... y cuarto.**
Es la una y cuarto.	1:15 / 13:15
Son las cuatro y cuarto.	4:15 / 16:15

- For other times past the hour, use **Son/Es la(s) ... y ...**
Es la una y veinte.	1:20 / 13:20
Son las cuatro y cinco.	4:05 / 16:05
Son las cinco y diez.	5:10 / 17:10

- For quarter to the hour, use **Son/Es la(s) ... menos cuarto.**
Es la una menos cuarto.	12:45 / 00:45
Son las cuatro menos cuarto.	3:45 / 15:45

• For other times to the hour, use **Son/Es la(s) … menos …**

Es la una menos veinticinco.	12:35 / 00:35
Son las once menos veinte.	10:40 / 22:40

If you want to ask and give the time, use **¿Qué hora es?**
The response will be **Es la … / Son las …**
Es la … is used for one o'clock (singular) only.
For all other times, use **Son las …**
Es la una y cinco.
Son las tres menos diez.
La(s) is used because the word **hora(s)** is understood, but not stated.

If you want to ask what time something happens, use **¿A qué hora … ?**
¿A qué hora sale el autobús?
What time does the bus leave?
¿A qué hora llega el autobús?
What time does the bus arrive?

Days and months

Capital letters are not used for months or days of the week in Spanish.

Days of the week

lunes	*Monday*
martes	*Tuesday*
miércoles	*Wednesday*
jueves	*Thursday*
viernes	*Friday*
sábado	*Saturday*
domingo	*Sunday*

Months of the year

enero	*January*
febrero	*February*
marzo	*March*
abril	*April*
mayo	*May*
junio	*June*
julio	*July*
agosto	*August*
septiembre (also: setiembre)	*September*
octubre	*October*
noviembre	*November*
diciembre	*December*

Notice that to say the date, you use **el** + day of the month + **de** + month + **de** + year:
el 2 de diciembre de 2005

If the date includes the day of the week, **el** is not used:
lunes, 29 de abril de 2004

SPANISH-ENGLISH WORDLIST

These wordlists give the Spanish words and phrases appearing in the course in alphabetical order (Spanish–English, English–Spanish), together with the unit number in which they are first presented.

A

a	to	7
a la plancha	grilled	5
a la romana	battered	5
a menudo	often	9
a pie	on foot	6
a veces	sometimes	9
abogado/a *(m/f)*	lawyer	2
abrigo *(m)*	coat	4
abril *(m)*	April	7
abuela *(f)*	grandmother	3
abuelo *(m)*	grandfather	3
aceite *(m)*	oil	4
aceitunas *(fpl)*	olives	5
acostarse	to go to bed	9
Adiós.	Goodbye.	1
adobado/a	seasoned, prepared	5
agosto *(m)*	August	7
agua caliente/		
fría *(f)*	hot/cold water	8
ahora	now	7
aire		
acondicionado *(m)*	air conditioning	8
ajo *(m)*	garlic	4
al final	at the end	6
al horno	in the oven	5
al lado de	next to, beside	6
albergue		
juvenil *(m)*	youth hostel	8

alcachofa *(f)*	artichoke	5
alcanzar	to reach, attain	10
alejarse (de)	to distance	
	oneself (from)	10
alemán (-ana)	German	1
¿Algo más?	Anything else?	4
algodón *(m)*	cotton	4
algunos/as	some	6
almejas *(fpl)*	clams	4
almendras *(fpl)*	almonds	5
alojamiento *(m)*	accommodation	9
alrededores *(mpl)*	surrounding area	6
alto/a	tall	3
amable	friendly	10
amarillo/a	yellow	4
amigo/a *(m/f)*	friend	3
ancho/a	loose	4
andando	walking, on foot	6
andar	to walk	6
andén *(m)*	platform	7
año *(m)*	year	2
el año pasado	last year	10
el año próximo	next year	9
el año que viene	next year	9
anoche	last night	10
anteayer	the day before	
	yesterday	10
antes	before	9
antipático/a	unkind, nasty	3

aparcamiento *(m)*	car park	9
apartamento *(m)*	apartment, flat	9
apellido *(m)*	surname	1
apetecer	to appeal to, fancy	5
aquél/aquélla/		
aquéllos/aquéllas	that (one) /those	
	(ones) (over there)	4
aquel/aquella/		
aquellos/aquellas	that/those (over	
	there)	4
aquí	here	4
Argentina	Argentina	2
argentino/a	Argentinian	2
armario *(m)*	cupboard	4
arquitecto/a *(m/f)*	architect	1
arreglarse	to get ready	9
arroz *(m)*	rice	4
asadillo *(m)*	roasted peppers	5
asado/a	roast(ed)	5
ascensor *(m)* (Sp)	lift	8
asunto *(m)*	subject	8
aterrizar	to land	7
atún *(m)*	tuna	4
autobús *(m)*	bus, coach	7
avión *(m)*	plane	7
ayer	yesterday	10
ayuntamiento *(m)*	town hall	6
azúcar *(m)*	sugar	4
azul	blue	3

B

bacalao (m)	cod	4
bailar	to dance	10
bajo/a	short (height)	3
baloncesto (m)	basketball	10
banco (m)	bank	6
baño (m)	bath	8
bar (m)	bar	2
barato/a	cheap, inexpensive	4
barba (f)	beard	3
barra (f)	loaf	4
berenjena (f)	aubergine	5
besugo (m)	sea bream	5
biblioteca (f)	library	6
bien	well	1
bienvenido/a	welcome	9
bigote (m)	moustache	3
billete (m) (Sp)	ticket	7
blanco/a	white	4
bola (f)	scoop	5
boleto (m) (LA)	ticket	7
Bolivia	Bolivia	2
boliviano/a	Bolivian	2
bolsa (f)	bag	4
botas (fpl)	boots	4
bote (m)	jar	4
botella (f)	bottle	4
Brasil	Brazil	2
brasileño/a	Brazilian	2
bucear	to scuba dive	10
Buen provecho.	Enjoy your meal.	5
Buenas noches.	Good night.	1
Buenas tardes.	Good afternoon.	1
bueno/a	good	3
Buenos días.	Good morning. / Hello.	1

C

cadena (f)	chain	8
café (m)	coffee	4
calabacín (m)	courgette	5
calamares (mpl)	squid	4
calefacción (f)	heating	8
calle (f)	street	6
calvo/a	bald	3
cama (f)	bed	8
cama de matrimonio (f)	double bed	8

camarero/a (m/f)	waiter/waitress	2
cambio (m)	change	5
camisa (f)	shirt	4
camping (m)	campsite	9
Canadá	Canada	2
canadiense	Canadian	2
canoso/a	grey(-haired)	3
cantante (m/f)	singer	2
carnet (de identidad) (m)	identity card	8
carnicería (f)	butcher's	4
caro/a	expensive	4
casado/a	married	3
casarse	to get married	10
casero/a	homemade, of the house	5
casi siempre	almost always	9
castaño/a	chestnut	3
castellano/a	Castilian	2
catalán (-ana)	Catalan	2
catalán (m)	Catalán (language)	2
catedral (f)	cathedral	6
cebolla (f)	onion	4
cenar	to have dinner	5
cenar fuera	to go out for dinner	5
céntimo (m)	cent	4
cerca de	near	6
cerdo (m)	pork	4
cerveza (f)	beer	4
champiñones (mpl)	mushrooms	4
chaqueta (f)	jacket	4
charcutería (f)	delicatessen/ cold meats	4
chile (m)	chilli	5
chino/a	Chinese	2
chocolate (m)	(hot) chocolate	5
chorizo (m)	spicy sausage	4
chuleta (f)	chop	5
cine (m)	cinema	9
ciudad (f)	city	6
clase (f)	class	9
clásico/a	classical	4
clasificar	to organise, sort	9
clínica (f)	clinic, surgery	2
coche (m)	car	7
cochinillo (m)	pork loin	5
cocina (f)	kitchen; cooker	8
código postal (m)	postcode	1
coger	to catch, take	6

col (f)	cabbage	5
colaborar (con)	to collaborate, work (with)	10
colegio (m)	school	2
colombiano/a	Colombian	2
comedor (m)	dining room	8
comer	to eat, have lunch	5
comer fuera	to go out for lunch	5
cómo	how	
¿Cómo está?	How are you? (formal)	1
¿Cómo estás?	How are you? (informal)	1
¿Cómo puedo ir a … ?	How do I get to…?	7
¿Cómo se escribe … ?	How do you spell …?	1
¿Cómo se llama?	What's your name? (formal)	1
cómodo/a	comfortable	7
comprar	to buy	4
con vista al mar	with a sea view	9
concierto (m)	concert	9
conmigo	with me	2
conocer	to know, meet, get to know	8
conocido/a	person you know	10
conseguir	to get, obtain	10
consultar	to consult	9
contable (m)	accountant	2
contestar	to answer	9
contigo	with you	2
copa (f)	wine glass	5
cordero (m)	lamb	4
correo electrónico (m)	e-mail	8
correos (m)	post office	6
correr	to run	10
correspondencia (f)	correspondence	9
cortado (m)	coffee with a dash of milk	5
corto/a	short (length)	3
costar (cuesta(n))	to cost	4
costumbre (f)	custom	9
Creo que …	I believe/think that …	8
croqueta (f)	croquette	5
crudo/a	raw	5

cruzar	to cross	6
cuadra *(f)* (LA)	block	6
¿Cuál es …?	What is …?	1
¿Cuánto es todo?	How much is it altogether?	4
cuántos	how many	2
¿Cuántos años tiene(s)?	How old are you?	2
cuarto *(m)*	room	8
cuarto de baño *(m)*	bathroom	8
cuarto de kilo	a quarter of a kilo	4
Cuba	Cuba	2
cubano/a	Cuban	2
cuenta *(f)*	bill	5
cuero *(m)*	leather	4
Cuesta creer.	It's hard to believe.	9

D

dar un paseo	to go for a walk	10
de	from, of	1
de cabrales	goat's	5
de cuadros	checked	4
¿De dónde eres?	Where are you from? (informal)	2
¿De dónde es?	Where are you from? (formal)	1
de ida	one way / single	7
de ida y vuelta	return	7
de la casa	house	5
de listas	striped	4
de lunares	spotted	4
de rayas	striped	4
de vez en cuando	from time to time	9
debajo de	under	6
deberes *(mpl)*	homework	10
débil	weak	3
decidir	to decide	10
decir	to say	10
del día	of the day	5
del tiempo	of the season	5
delante de	in front of	6
delgado/a	slim	3
demasiado/a	too (much/many)	10
deporte *(m)*	sport	9
derecha; a la derecha	right; on the right	6

desayunar	to have breakfast	9
descansar	to rest	9
desde	from	7
desear	to wish, want	4
despacho *(m)*	office	9
después	after	9
destino *(m)*	destination	7
detrás de	behind	6
día *(m)*	day	7
diciembre *(m)*	December	7
dirección *(f)*	address	1
director(a) *(m/f)*	director	2
discoteca *(f)*	disco, club	10
divertido/a	funny, amusing	10
divorciado/a	divorced	3
divorciarse	to get divorced	10
doblar	to turn	6
doble	double	8
doble habitación	double room	10
domingo *(m)*	Sunday	7
dónde	where	2
dormirse	to fall asleep	9
dormitorio *(m)*	bedroom	8
ducha *(f)*	shower	8
ducharse	to have a shower	9

E

echar cabezadas	to have a snooze, nod off	9
echarse la siesta	to take a nap	9
Edimburgo	Edinburgh	1
el	the	1
él	he	1
elegante	elegant	8
elevador *(m)* (LA)	lift	8
ella	she	1
empanada *(f)*	meat or fish pie	5
empezar	to start	9
en	in, on	1,7
en el centro	in the centre/middle	6
en la esquina	on the corner	6
en primer lugar	firstly	9
en punto	precisely, on the dot	7
Encantado/a.	Pleased to meet you.	1
encantar	to love, like very much	5

encima de	on top of	6
encontrar	to meet, find	9
enero *(m)*	January	7
enfermero/a *(m/f)*	nurse	2
enfrente de	opposite	6
ensalada *(f)*	salad	5
entrada *(f)*	(entrance) ticket	7
entre … y …	between … and …	6
equipo *(m)*	team	10
¿Es directo?	Is it direct?	7
Es la una.	It's one o'clock.	7
escaparate *(m)*	shop window	4
escuchar	to listen (to)	9
ese/esa/esos/esas	that/those	4
ése/ésa/ésos/ésas	that (one) / those (ones)	4
español(a)	Spanish	1
espinacas *(fpl)*	spinach	5
esquí *(m)*	skiing	10
esquiar	to ski, go skiing	9
Está nublado.	It's cloudy.	6
estación de tren/ autobús *(f)*	train/bus station	6
Estados Unidos *(mpl)*	the United States	4
estadounidense	American, from the USA	1
estampado/a	patterned	4
estanco *(m)*	tobacconist's	4
estantería *(f)*	shelves	8
estar	to be	3
estar en rebajas	to be in a sale	4
este *(m)*	east	6
este/esta/estos/ estas	this/these	4
éste/ésta/éstos/ éstas	this (one) / these (ones)	4
estrecho/a	tight	4
estudiante *(m/f)*	student	1
estudiar	to study	9
euro *(m)*	euro	4
examen *(m)*	exam	9
excursión *(f)*	excursion	9
exposición *(f)*	exhibition	9
extrovertido/a	outgoing	3

F

factura (f)	bill, invoice	8
falda (f)	skirt	4
familia (f)	family	3
farmacia (f)	chemist's	4
fatal	terrible	1
febrero (m)	February	7
fecha (f)	date	8
feo/a	ugly	3
fiesta (f)	party	10
filete (m)	fillet	5
Filipinas	the Philippines	2
filipino/a	Philippino	2
fin de semana (m)	weekend	9
finalmente	finally	9
firmar	to sign	8
flan (m)	crème caramel	5
francés (-esa)	French	1
Francia (f)	France	2
fregadero (m)	(kitchen) sink	8
fresa (f)	strawberry	5
frigorífico (m)	fridge	4
frío/a	cold	8
frito/a	fried	5
fruta (f)	fruit	4
frutería (f)	fruit shop	4
fuerte	strong	3
fumador / no fumador	smoking/non smoking	7
fútbol (m)	football	9

G

gafas (fpl)	glasses	3
gallego/a	Galician	2
galletas (fpl)	biscuits	4
gambas (fpl)	prawns	4
ganar	to win	10
generoso/a	generous	3
gente (f)	people	10
gimnasio (m)	gym	9
gordo/a	fat	3
Gracias.	Thank you.	1
gramo (m)	gram	4
grande	big	3
gratinado/a	with grated cheese	5
gris	grey	3,4
guapo/a	pretty, good-looking	3
guía (m/f)	guide	9

guisantes (mpl)	peas	4
gustar	to like	5

H

habitación (f)	room	8
hablar	to talk, speak	2
Hace buen tiempo.	The weather's nice.	6
Hace calor.	It's hot.	6
Hace fresco.	It's chilly.	6
Hace frío.	It's cold.	6
Hace mal tiempo.	The weather's bad.	6
Hace sol.	It's sunny.	6
hace unos días	a few days ago	10
Hace viento.	It's windy.	6
hacer juego	to match, go together	4
hamaca (f)	deckchair	9
harina (f)	flour	5
hasta	until	7
¿Hay … ?	Is/Are there …?	6
hecho/a	done, prepared	5
helado (m)	ice cream	5
hermana (f)	sister	3
hermano (m)	brother	3
hija (f)	daughter	3
hijo (m)	son	3
hijos (mpl)	children	3
historia (f)	history, story	10
¡Hola!	Hello!	1
hospital (m)	hospital	2
hoy	today	7
huevo (m)	egg	4

I

ibérico/a	Iberian	5
iglesia (f)	church	6
ilustre	famous, illustrious	10
inaugurar	to inaugurate	10
incluir	to include	9
increíble	incredible, unbelievable	9
individual	single	8
inglés (-esa)	English	1
insensible	insensitive	3
instalaciones (fpl)	facilities	8
invitado/a (m/f)	guest	10
ir	to go	
ir a juego	to match, go together	4
ir a la moda	to be fashionable	4

ir de copas	to go for a drink	9
ir de escaparates	to go window-shopping	4
ir de excursión	to go on a trip	10
ir de tapas	to go for tapas	5
ir de vacaciones	to go on holiday	9
ir de vinos	to go for a drink	9
irresponsable	irresponsible	3
Italia	Italy	2
italiano/a	Italian	1
itinerario (m)	itinerary	9
izquierda; a la izquierda	left; on the left	6

J

jamón (m)	ham	4
Japón	Japan	2
japonés (-esa)	Japanese	2
jardín (m)	garden	9
jersey (m)	sweater	4
judías verdes (fpl)	green beans	4
jueves (m)	Thursday	7
jugar	to play	9
julio (m)	July	7
junio (m)	June	7
junto/a	together	10

K

kilo (m)	kilo	4
kilómetro (m)	kilometre	6

L

lácteos (mpl)	dairy products	4
lámpara (f)	lamp	8
lana (f)	wool	4
largo/a	long	3
lata (f)	tin, can	4
lavabo (m)	washbasin	8
lavadora (f)	washing machine	8
lavarse	to wash (oneself)	9
lavavajillas (m)	dishwasher	8
leche (f)	milk	4
lechuga (f)	lettuce	4
lejos (de)	far (from)	6
lenguado (m)	sole	5
levantarse	to get up	9
libre	free, available	5

Spanish	English	
libro de reclamaciones (m)	complaints book	8
licor (m)	liqueur	5
lino (m)	linen	4
liquidación (f)	sale	4
liso/a	straight	3
listo/a	clever	3
litro (m)	litre	4
llamar por teléfono	to phone	9
llamarse	to be called	1
llegada (f)	arrival	7
llegar (a)	to reach, arrive (at)	7
llevar	to wear, take, carry, contain	4
llover	to rain	6
lluvia (f)	rain	6
Lo siento.	I'm sorry.	5
lo/la/los/las	him/her/it/them	4
Londres	London	1
luego	then	9
lunes (m)	Monday	7

M

Spanish	English	
macedonia (f)	fruit salad	5
madre (f)	mother	3
mal	not too good	1
malo/a	bad	3
mañana	tomorrow	7
mantequilla (f)	butter	4
manzana (f)	apple	4
manzana (f) (Sp)	block	6
maratón (f)	marathon	10
marido (m)	husband	3
mariscos (mpl)	seafood	5
marrón (-ones)	brown	3,4
martes (m)	Tuesday	7
marzo (m)	March	7
más que	more than	6
matemáticas (fpl)	maths	9
mayo (m)	May	7
mecánico/a (m/f)	mechanic	1
media pensión	half board	8
médico (m)	doctor	2
medio kilo	half a kilo	4
mejillones (mpl)	mussels	4
menos cuarto	quarter to	7

Spanish	English	
menos que	less than	6
mentiroso/a	lying, a liar	3
menú (m)	menu	5
mercado (m)	market	9
merluza (f)	hake	4
mermelada (f)	jam	4
mes (m)	month	7
el mes pasado	last month	10
el mes próximo	next month	9
el mes que viene	next month	9
mesilla de noche (f)	bedside table	8
metro (m)	underground station	6
mexicano/a	Mexican	2
mi	my	3
miércoles (m)	Wednesday	7
mini-bar (m)	minibar	8
mirar	to look (at)	7
mito (m)	myth, legend	9
mixto/a	mixed	5
montar a caballo	to go horseriding	10
montar en bicicleta	to ride a bike	10
monumento (m)	monument	7
moreno/a	dark	3
morir	to die	10
Mucho gusto.	Pleased to meet you.	3
muchos/as	many	6
mujer (f)	woman, wife	3
música (clásica) (f)	(classical) music	9
muy bien	very well	1

N

Spanish	English	
nacer	to be born	10
nacionalidad (f)	nationality	1
nadar	to swim	9
naranja	orange (coloured)	4
naranja (f)	orange	4
nata (f)	cream	5
Navidad (f)	Christmas	10
negro/a	black	3
nervioso/a	nervous	3
nevar	to snow	6
nieta (f)	granddaughter	3
nieto (m)	grandson	3
nieve (f)	snow	6

Spanish	English	
no	no	1
nombre (m)	(first) name	1
normalmente	normally	9
norte (m)	north	6
nota (f)	note	9
noviembre (m)	November	7
nuestro/a	our	8
nunca	never	9

O

Spanish	English	
octubre (m)	October	7
oeste (m)	west	6
oferta (f)	offer	4
oficina (f)	office	2
oficina de información (f)	tourist information office	6
oficinista (m/f)	office worker, clerk	2
¡Oiga!	Excuse me!	5
optimista	optimistic	3
ordenado/a	organized	9
organizar	to organize	9
otoño (m)	autumn	6

P

Spanish	English	
padre (m)	father	3
paella (valenciana) (f)	paella	5
pan (m)	bread	4
panadería (f)	baker's	4
pantalones (mpl)	trousers	4
papel higiénico (m)	toilet paper	8
papelería (f)	stationer's	4
paquete (m)	packet	4
para	for	4,7
Para mí.	For me.	5
parecer	to seem, appear	9
París	Paris	1
parque (m)	park	6
pasado mañana	the day after tomorrow	9
pasear	to walk, stroll	10
pasillo (m)	corridor	8
patinar	to skate	10
patio (m)	patio	9
pechuga de pollo (f)	chicken breast	5

pedir	to ask for	10
película (f)	film	9
pelirrojo/a	red-haired	3
pensión completa	full board	8
pepino (m)	cucumber	4
pequeño/a	small	3
pera (f)	pear	4
¿Perdón?	Pardon?	1
perezoso/a	lazy	3
periódico (m)	newspaper	4
pero	but	2
pescadería (f)	fishmonger's	4
pesimista	pessimistic	3
pez espada (m)	swordfish	5
piano (m)	piano	10
piel (f)	leather, skin	4
Pienso que …	I think that …	8
pimienta (f)	pepper (condiment)	4
pimiento (m)	pepper (vegetable)	4
piscina (f)	swimming pool	6
piscina municipal (f)	(council) swimming pool	10
piso (m)	flat	9
pista de patinaje (f)	ice rink	10
placer (m)	pleasure	8
planear	to plan	9
plátano (m)	banana	4
plaza (f)	square	6
pobre	poor	3
poder	to be able to, can	5
pollo (m)	chicken	4
pomelo (m)	grapefruit	4
poner	to put	10
por	for, through, along	7
por aquí	around/near here	6
por la mañana	in the morning	7
por la noche	at night	7
por la tarde	in the afternoon/ evening	7
por lo general	usually, in general	9
portugués (-esa)	Portuguese	2
posguerra (f)	postwar	10
postre (m)	dessert	5
Prefiero …	I prefer …	4
preparar	to prepare	9
prima (f)	(female) cousin	3
primavera (f)	spring	6

primer plato (m)	first course	5
primo (m)	(male) cousin	3
probar	to try	4
procedencia de	coming from	7
profesión (f)	profession	1
profesor(a) (m/f)	teacher	1
propina (f)	tip	5
provincia (f)	province, county	1
próximo/a (m/f)	next one	7
pueblo (m)	town, village	6
¿Puede repetir, por favor?	Can you repeat, please?	1
puerta (f)	gate, door	7
pulpo (m)	octopus	5
púrpura	purple	4

Q

qué	what	2
¿Qué desea?	What would you like?	4
¿Qué hace(s)?	What do you do?	2
¡Qué pena!	What a shame!	4
¿Qué tal?	How are you? (informal)	1
quedar	to stay	9
quedar con alguien	to arrange to meet someone	9
querer	to want	4
queso (m)	cheese	4
quiosco (m)	kiosk, newspaper stand	4
Quisiera …	I would like …	4

R

ración (f)	portion	5
radio (f)	radio	10
rápido/a	fast, quick	7
realizar	to do, carry out	9
rebajas (fpl)	sales	4
rebozado/a	rolled in (breadcrumbs)	5
recepción (f)	reception	2
recepcionista (m/f)	receptionist	2
recoger	to meet, collect	7
regalo (m)	present	9
regatear	to bargain, haggle	4
regular	so-so	1

relleno/a	stuffed	5
reserva (f)	reservation, booking	9
reservada/o	reserved, booked	5
responsable	responsible	3
restaurante (m)	restaurant	8
retraso (m)	delay	7
reunión (f)	meeting	9
revista (f)	magazine	4
revuelto (m)	scrambled eggs	5
rico/a	rich	3
rizado/a	curly	3
rojo/a	red	3
Roma	Rome	1
romper	to break	9
rosa	pink	4
rubio/a	blonde, fair	3
Rusia	Russia	2
ruso/a	Russian	2

S

sábado (m)	Saturday	7
saber	to know	10
sal (f)	salt	4
salado/a	salted	5
salchichón (m)	salami	4
salida (f)	departure	7
salir (de)	to leave	7
salmón (m)	salmon	4
salón (m)	living room	8
salón de reuniones (m)	meeting room	8
sandalias (fpl)	sandals	4
se alquila	to let	9
se compra	wanted (to buy)	9
se vende	for sale	9
secretario/a (m/f)	secretary	2
seda (f)	silk	4
seguidamente	then, next	9
seguir	to follow	6
segundo plato (m)	second/main course	5
semana (f)	week	7
la semana pasada	last week	10
la semana próxima	next week	9
la semana que viene	next week	9
señor (m)	sir, Mr	1
señora (f)	madam, Mrs	1
señorita (f)	miss, Miss	1
sensible	sensitive	3

septiembre (m)	September	7
ser	to be	1
ser una ganga	to be a bargain	4
servicios (mpl)	services; toilets	8
setas (fpl)	wild mushrooms	5
sí	yes	1
siempre	always	9
sierra (f)	mountain range	9
siesta (f)	nap	9
siguiente	following	10
silla (f)	chair	8
sillón (m)	armchair	8
simpático/a	nice, kind	3
sincero/a	sincere, honest	3
sobre (las ocho)	about, around (eight o'clock)	9
sobrina (f)	niece	3
sobrino (m)	nephew	3
sofá (m)	sofa	8
soler	to be in the habit of, usually do	9
solicitar	to ask for	8
soltero/a	single	3
Son las …	It's … o'clock.	7
sopa (f)	soup	5
su	your (formal)	1
su	his/her/its/your	3
sucio/a	dirty	8
sur (m)	south	6

T

tabla de quesos (f)	cheeseboard	5
tacaño/a	mean, stingy	3
talla (f)	size	4
también	also	2
tan … como	as … as	6
tanto … como	as … as	6
tarde	late	9
taxi (m)	taxi	10
taxista (m/f)	taxi driver	2
té (m)	tea	4
teatro (m)	theatre	6
tela (f)	material, fabric	4
teléfono (m)	telephone (number)	1
televisión (f)	TV	8
temprano	early	9
tener	to have	2

tener marcha	to be energetic	10
¿Tengo que bajar en …?	Do I have to get off at …?	7
¿Tengo que hacer transbordo?	Do I have to change?	7
tercero/a	third	6
terminar	to finish	9
ternera (f)	veal	4
terraza (f)	terrace	9
tía (f)	aunt	3
tienda (f)	shop	6
tienda de comestibles (f)	grocer's	4
tienda de moda (f)	clothes shop	4
¿Tiene …?	Does it/he/she/you have …?	6
tímido/a	shy	3
tío (m)	uncle	3
típico/a	typical	5
toalla (f)	towel	8
tocar	to play (an instrument)	10
todo recto	straight on	6
tomar	to take, eat, drink	5,6
tomar el aperitivo	to have an aperitif/drink	9
tomar el sol	to sunbathe	9
tomate (m)	tomato	4
tonto/a	stupid	3
torcer	to turn	6
tortilla (de patatas) (f)	(potato) omelette	5
trabajador(a)	hard-working	3
trabajar	to work	2
traer	to bring	10
tranquilo/a	calm	3
traslado (m)	transfer	9
tren (m)	train	7
tribunal (m)	lawyer's office	2
tu	your (informal)	1
tú	you (informal)	1
tutear	to call someone tú	2

U

último/a	last	7

universidad (f)	university	9
usted	you (formal)	1
uvas (fpl)	grapes	4
vacaciones (fpl)	holiday	9

V

Vale.	OK.	4
Vamos a hablar.	Let's talk.	9
¡Vamos a ver!	Let's see. / We'll see.	9
vaqueros (mpl)	jeans	4
variado/a	varied, different	5
varios/as	various, several	6
vascuence (m)	Basque (language)	2
vaso (m)	glass	8
vender	to sell	4
venir	to come	7
ver	to see	9
verano (m)	summer	6
verde	green	3
verduras (fpl)	vegetables	4
vermut (m)	vermouth	5
vestirse	to get dressed	9
vez (f)	time, occasion	9
una vez / dos/tres veces	once / twice/three times	9
vía	via, by way of	7
vía (f)	platform	7
viaje (m)	journey	9
viernes (m)	Friday	7
vinagre (m)	vinegar	5
vino blanco (m)	white wine	4
vino tinto (m)	red wine	4
visita (f)	visit	9
visitar	to visit	7
viudo/a	widowed	3
vivir	to live	1
volver (a)	to go back, return (to)	9
vuestro/a	your	8

W, Y, Z

wáter (m)	toilet	8
y cuarto	quarter past	7
y media	half past	7
yo	I	1
yogur (m)	yoghurt	4
zumo (m)	juice	5

ENGLISH-SPANISH WORDLIST

A

a few days ago	hace unos días	10
a quarter of		
a kilo	cuarto kilo	4
about, around		
(eight o'clock)	sobre (las ocho)	9
accommodation	alojamiento (m)	9
accountant	contable (m)	2
address	dirección (f)	1
after	después	9
air conditioning	aire acondicionado (m)	8
almonds	almendras (fpl)	5
almost always	casi siempre	9
also	también	2
always	siempre	9
American, from		
the USA	estadounidense	1
answer, to	contestar	9
Anything else?	¿Algo más?	4
apartment, flat	apartamento (m)	9
appeal to, to	apetecer	5
appear, to	parecer	9
apple	manzana (f)	4
April	abril (m)	7
architect	arquitecto/a (m/f)	1
Argentina	Argentina (f)	2
Argentinian	argentino/a	2
armchair	sillón (m)	8
around/near here	por aquí	6
arrange to meet		
someone, to	quedar con alguien	9
arrival	llegada (f)	7
arrive (at) , to	llegar (a)	7

artichoke	alcachofa (f)	5
as … as	tan … como/ tanto …	
	como	6
ask for, to	solicitar	8
ask for, to	pedir	10
at night	por la noche	7
at the end	al final	6
aubergine	berenjena (f)	5
August	agosto (m)	7
aunt	tía (f)	3
autumn	otoño (m)	6
available	libre	5

B

bad	malo/a	3
bag	bolsa (f)	4
baker's	panadería (f)	4
bald	calvo/a	3
banana	plátano (m)	4
bank	banco (m)	6
bar	bar (m)	2
bargain, to	regatear	4
basketball	baloncesto (m)	10
Basque		
(language)	vascuence (m)	2
bath	baño (m)	8
bathroom	cuarto de baño (m)	8
battered	a la romana	5
be, to	ser, estar	1,3
be a bargain, to	ser una ganga	4
be able to, to	poder	5
be born, to	nacer	10
be called, to	llamarse	1

be energetic, to	tener marcha	10
be fashionable,		
to	ir a la moda	4
be in a sale, to	estar en rebajas	4
be in the habit		
of, to	soler	9
beard	barba (f)	3
bed	cama (f)	8
bedroom	dormitorio (m)	8
bedside table	mesilla de noche (f)	8
beer	cerveza (f)	4
before	antes	9
behind	detrás de	6
between …		
and …	entre … y …	6
big	grande	3
bill	cuenta (f)	5
bill	factura (f)	8
biscuits	galletas (fpl)	4
black	negro/a	3,4
block	cuadra (f) (LA)	6
block	manzana (f) (Sp)	6
blonde	rubio/a	3
blue	azul	3,4
Bolivia	Bolivia (f)	2
Bolivian	boliviano/a	2
booked	reservada/o	5
booking	reserva (f)	9
boots	botas (fpl)	4
bottle	botella (f)	4
Brazil	Brasil (m)	2
Brazilian	brasileño/a	2
bread	pan (m)	4

break, to	romper	9	chilli	chile (m)	5	cross, to	cruzar	6
bring, to	traer	10	Chinese	chino/a	2	Cuba	Cuba (f)	2
brother	hermano (m)	3	chocolate	chocolate (m)	5	Cuban	cubano/a	2
brown	marrón	3,4	chop	chuleta (f)	5	cucumber	pepino (m)	4
bus	autobús (m)	7	Christmas	Navidad (f)	10	cupboard	armario (m)	4
bus station	estación de		church	iglesia (f)	6	curly	rizado/a	3
	autobús (f)	6	cinema	cine (m)	9	custom	costumbre (f)	9
but	pero	2	city	ciudad (f)	6			
butcher's	carnicería (f)	4	clams	almejas (fpl)	4			

C

butter	mantequilla (f)	4	class	clase (f)	9	dairy products	lácteos (mpl)	4
buy, to	comprar	4	classical	clásico/a	4	dance, to	bailar	10

C

			clerk	oficinista (m/f)	2	dark	moreno/a	3
cabbage	col (f)	5	clever	listo/a	3	date	fecha (f)	8
call someone tú	tú, tutear	2	clinic	clínica (f)	2	daughter	hija (f)	3
calm	tranquilo/a	3	clothes shop	tienda de moda (f)	4	day	día (m)	7
campsite	camping (m)	9	coach	autobús (m)	7	December	diciembre (m)	7
can (tin)	lata (f)	4	coat	abrigo (m)	4	decide, to	decidir	10
Can you			cod	bacalao (m)	4	deckchair	hamaca (f)	9
repeat, please?	¿Puede repetir,		coffee	café (m)	4	delay	retraso (m)	7
	por favor?	1	coffee with a			delicatessen/		
Canada	Canadá (m)	2	dash of milk	cortado (m)	5	cold meats	charcutería (f)	4
Canadian	canadiense	2	cold	frío/a	8	departure	salida (f)	7
car	coche (m)	7	cold water	agua fría (f)	8	dessert	postre (m)	5
car park	aparcamiento (m)	9	collaborate			destination	destino (m)	7
carry out, to	realizar	9	(with), to	colaborar (con)	10	die, to	morir	10
carry, to	llevar	4,5	Colombian	colombiano/a	2	different	variado/a	5
Castilian	castellano/a	2	come, to	venir	7	dining room	comedor (m)	8
Catalan	catalán (-ana)	2	comfortable	cómodo/a	7	director	director(a) (m/f)	2
Catalán			coming from	procedencia de	7	dirty	sucio/a	8
(language)	catalán (m)	2	complaints book	libro de		disco	discoteca (f)	10
				reclamaciones (m)	8	dishwasher	lavavajillas (m)	8
catch, to	coger	6	concert	concierto (m)	9	distance oneself		
cathedral	catedral (f)	6	consult, to	consultar	9	(from), to	alejarse (de)	10
cent	céntimo (m)	4	contain, to	llevar	4,5	divorced	divorciado/a	3
chain	cadena (f)	8	cooker	cocina (f)	8	Do I have to	¿Tengo que hacer	
chair	silla (f)	8	correspondence	correspondencia (f)	9	change?	transbordo?	7
change	cambio (m)	5	corridor	pasillo (m)	8	Do I have to	¿Tengo que	
cheap	barato/a	4	cost, to	costar (cuesta(n))	4	get off in ...?	bajar en ...?	7
checked	de cuadros	4	cotton	algodón (m)	4	doctor	médico (m)	2
cheese	queso (m)	4	county	provincia (f)	1	Does it/he/she/		
cheeseboard	tabla de quesos (f)	5	courgette	calabacín (m)	5	you have ...?	¿Tiene ...?	6
chemist's	farmacia (f)	4	cousin (female)	prima (f)	3	done	hecho/a	5
chestnut	castaño/a	3	cousin (male)	primo (m)	3	door	puerta (f)	7
chicken	pollo (m)	4	cream	nata (f)	5	double	doble	8
chicken breast	pechuga de pollo (f)	5	crème caramel	flan (m)	5	double bed	cama de matrimonio (f)	8
children	hijos (mpl)	3	croquette	croqueta (f)	5	double room	doble habitación	10

E

early	temprano	9
east	este (m)	6
eat, have lunch, to	comer	5
Edinburgh	Edimburgo	1
egg	huevo (m)	4
elegant	elegante	8
e-mail	correo electrónico (m)	8
English	inglés (-esa)	1
Enjoy your meal.	Buen provecho.	5
entrance ticket	entrada (f)	7
euro	euro (m)	4
exam	examen (m)	9
excursion	excursión (f)	9
Excuse me!	¡Oiga!	5
exhibition	exposición (f)	9
expensive	caro/a	4

F

fabric	tela (f)	4
facilities	instalaciones (fpl)	8
fair (hair)	rubio/a	3
fall asleep, to	dormirse	9
family	familia (f)	3
famous	ilustre	10
fancy, to	apetecer	5
far (from)	lejos (de)	6
fast	rápido/a	7
fat	gordo/a	3
father	padre (m)	3
February	febrero (m)	7
Filipino	filipino/a	2
fillet	filete (m)	5
film	película (f)	9
finally	finalmente	9
finish, to	terminar	9
first course	primer plato (m)	5
firstly	en primer lugar	9
fishmonger's	pescadería (f)	4
flat	piso (m)	9
flour	harina (f)	5
follow, to	seguir	6
following	siguiente	10
football	fútbol (m)	9
for	para	4,7
For me.	Para mí.	5
for sale	se vende	9

for, through, along	por	7
France	Francia (f)	2
free	libre	5
French	francés (a)	1
Friday	viernes (m)	7
fridge	frigorífico (m)	4
fried	frito/a	5
friend	amigo/a (m/f)	3
friendly	amable	10
from	desde	7
from	de	1,7
from time to time	de vez en cuando	9
fruit	fruta (f)	4
fruit salad	macedonia (f)	5
fruit shop	frutería (f)	4
full board	pensión completa	8
funny, amusing	divertido/a	10

G

Galician	gallego/a	2
garden	jardín (m)	9
garlic	ajo (m)	4
gate	puerta (f)	7
generous	generoso/a	3
German	alemán/a	1
get divorced, to	divorciarse	10
get dressed, to	vestirse	9
get married, to	casarse	10
get ready, to	arreglarse	9
get up, to	levantarse	9
get, obtain, to	conseguir	10
glass	vaso (m)	8
glasses	gafas (fpl)	3
go back, return, to	volver (a)	9
go for a drink, to	ir de copas	9
go for a drink, to	ir de vinos	9
go for a walk, to	dar un paseo	10
go on a trip, to	ir de excursión	10
go for tapas, to	ir de tapas	5
go horseriding, to	montar a caballo	10
go on holiday, to	ir de vacaciones	9
go out for dinner, to	cenar fuera	5
go out for lunch, to	comer fuera	5

go to bed, to	acostarse	9
go window-shopping, to	ir de escaparates	4
goat's	de cabrales	5
good	bueno/a	3
Good afternoon.	Buenas tardes.	1
Good morning. / Hello.	Buenos días.	1
Good night.	Buenas noches.	1
Goodbye.	Adiós.	1
good-looking	guapo/a	3
gram	gramo (m)	4
granddaughter	nieta (f)	3
grandfather	abuelo (m)	3
grandmother	abuela (f)	3
grandson	nieto (m)	3
grapefruit	pomelo (m)	4
grapes	uvas (fpl)	4
green	verde	3,4
green beans	judías verdes (fpl)	4
grey	gris	3,4
grey(-haired)	canoso/a	3
grilled	a la plancha	5
grocer's	tienda de comestibles (f)	4
guest	invitado/a (m/f)	10
guide	guía (m/f)	9
gym	gimnasio (m)	9

H

haggle, to	regatear	4
hake	merluza (f)	4
half a kilo	medio kilo	4
half board	media pensión	8
half past	y media	7
ham	jamón (m)	4
hard-working	trabajador(a)	3
have a shower, to	ducharse	9
have a snooze, nod off, to	echar cabezadas	9
have an aperitif/ drink, to	tomar el aperitivo	9
have breakfast, to	desayunar	9
have dinner, to	cenar	5
have, to	tener	2
he	él	1
heating	calefacción (f)	8

English	Spanish	
Hello!	¡Hola!	1
her	su	3
here	aquí	4
his	su	3
history	historia *(f)*	10
holiday	vacaciones *(fpl)*	9
homemade, of the house	casero/a	5
homework	deberes *(mpl)*	10
honest	sincero/a	3
hospital	hospital *(m)*	2
hot chocolate	chocolate *(m)*	5
hot water	agua caliente *(f)*	8
house	de la casa	5
How are you? (formal)	¿Cómo está?	1
How are you? (informal)	¿Cómo estás?	1
How are you? (informal)	¿Qué tal?	1
How do I get to …?	¿Cómo puedo ir a … ?	7
How do you spell …?	¿Cómo se escribe … ?	1
how many	cuántos	2
How much is it altogether?	¿Cuánto es todo?	4
How old are you?	¿Cuántos años tiene(s)?	2
husband	marido *(m)*	3

I

I	yo	1
I believe/think that …	Creo que …	8
I prefer …	Prefiero …	4
I think that …	Pienso que …	8
I would like …	Quisiera …	4
I'm sorry.	Lo siento.	5
Iberian	ibérico/a	5
ice cream	helado *(m)*	5
ice rink	pista de patinaje *(f)*	10
identity card	carnet (de identidad) *(m)*	8
illustrious	ilustre	10
in front of	delante de	6
in the afternoon/		

evening	por la tarde	7
in the centre/ middle	en el centro	6
in the morning	por la mañana	7
in the oven	al horno	5
in, on	en	1,7
inaugurate, to	inaugurar	10
include, to	incluir	9
incredible	increíble	9
inexpensive	barato/a	4
insensitive	insensible	3
invoice	factura *(f)*	8
irresponsible	irresponsable	3
Is it direct?	¿Es directo?	7
Is/Are there …?	¿Hay … ?	6
it/them	lo/la/los/las	4
It's … o'clock.	Son las …	7
It's chilly.	Hace fresco.	6
It's cloudy.	Está nublado.	6
It's cold.	Hace frío.	6
It's hard to believe.	Cuesta creer.	9
It's hot.	Hace calor.	6
It's one o'clock.	Es la una.	7
It's sunny.	Hace sol.	6
It's windy.	Hace viento.	6
Italian	italiano/a	1
Italy	Italia *(f)*	2
itinerary	itinerario *(m)*	9

J

jacket	chaqueta *(f)*	4
jam	mermelada *(f)*	4
January	enero *(m)*	7
Japan	Japón *(m)*	2
Japanese	japonés (-esa)	2
jar	bote *(m)*	4
jeans	vaqueros *(mpl)*	4
journey	viaje *(m)*	9
juice	zumo *(m)*	5
July	julio *(m)*	7
June	junio *(m)*	7

K

kilo	kilo *(m)*	4
kilometre	kilómetro *(m)*	6
kind	simpático/a	3

kiosk	quiosco *(m)*	4
kitchen	cocina *(f)*	8
know, to	saber	10
know, to (someone)	conocer	8
known	conocido	10

L

lamb	cordero *(m)*	4
lamp	lámpara *(f)*	8
land, to	aterrizar	7
last	último/a	7
last month	el mes pasado	10
last night	anoche	10
last week	la semana pasada	10
last year	el año pasado	10
late	tarde	9
lawyer	abogado/a *(m/f)*	2
lawyer's office	tribunal *(m)*	2
lazy	perezoso/a	3
leather	cuero *(m)*	4
leather, skin	piel *(f)*	4
leave, to	salir *(de)*	7,9
left; on the left	izquierda; a la izquierda	6
legend	mito *(m)*	9
less than	menos que	6
let, to	se alquila	9
Let's see. / We'll see.	Vamos a ver!	9
Let's talk.	Vamos a hablar.	9
lettuce	lechuga *(f)*	4
library	biblioteca *(f)*	6
lift	ascensor *(m)* (Sp)	8
lift	elevador *(m)* (LA)	8
like, to	gustar *(imp.)*	5
linen	lino *(m)*	4
liqueur	licor *(m)*	5
listen (to), to	escuchar	9
litre	litro *(m)*	4
live, to	vivir	1
living room	salón *(m)*	8
loaf	barra *(f)*	4
London	Londres	1
long	largo/a	3
look (at), to	mirar	7
loose	ancho/a	4

love, like very much, to	encantar	5
lying	mentiroso/a	3

M

madam, Mrs	señora (f)	1
magazine	revista (f)	4
many	muchos/as	6
marathon	maratón (f)	10
March	marzo (m)	7
market	mercado (m)	9
married	casado/a	3
match, go together, to	hacer juego	4
match, go together, to	ir a juego	4
material	tela (f)	4
maths	matemáticas (fpl)	9
May	mayo (m)	7
mean	tacaño/a	3
meat or fish pie	empanada (f)	5
mechanic	mecánico/a (m/f)	1
meet, collect, to	recoger	7
meet, find, to	encontrar	9
meeting	reunión (f)	9,10
meeting room	salón de reuniones (m)	8
menu	menú (m)	5
Mexican	mexicano/a	2
milk	leche (f)	4
minibar	mini-bar (m)	8
miss, Miss	señorita (f)	1
mixed	mixto/a	5
Monday	lunes (m)	7
month	mes (m)	7
monument	monumento (m)	7
more than	más que	6
mother	madre (f)	3
mountain range	sierra (f)	9
moustache	bigote (m)	3
mushrooms	champiñones (mpl)	4
music (classical)	música (clásica) (f)	9
mussels	mejillones (mpl)	4
my	mi	3
myth	mito (m)	9

N

name (first)	nombre (m)	1
nap	siesta (f)	9
narrow	ancho/a	4

nasty	antipático/a	3
nationality	nacionalidad (f)	1
near	cerca de	6
nephew	sobrino (m)	3
nervous	nervioso/a	3
never	nunca	9
newspaper	periódico (m)	4
newspaper stand	quiosco (m)	4
next month	el mes próximo	9
next month	el mes que viene	9
next one	próximo/a (m/f)	7
next to, beside	al lado de	6
next week	la semana próxima	9
next week	la semana que viene	9
next year	el año próximo	9
next year	el año que viene	9
nice	simpático/a	3
niece	sobrina (f)	3
no	no	1
non smoking	no fumador	7
normally	normalmente	9
north	norte (m)	6
not too good	mal	1
note	nota (f)	9
November	noviembre (m)	7
now	ahora	7
nurse	enfermero/a (m/f)	2

O

October	octubre (m)	7
octopus	pulpo (m)	5
of	de	1,7
of the day	del día	5
of the season	del tiempo	5
offer	oferta (f)	4
office	despacho (m)	9
office worker	oficinista (m/f)	2
oficina	oficina (f)	2
often	a menudo	9
oil	aceite (m)	4
OK.	Vale.	4
olives	aceitunas (fpl)	5
omelette (potato)	tortilla (de patatas) (f)	5
on foot	a pie	6
on the corner	en la esquina	6
on top of	encima de	6
once / twice / three times	una vez / dos/tres veces	9
one way	de ida	7

onion	cebolla (f)	4
opposite	enfrente de	6
optimistic	optimista	3
orange	naranja (f)	4
orange (coloured)	naranja	4
organize, to	organizar	9
organized	ordenado/a	9
our	nuestro/a	8
outgoing	extrovertido/a	3

P

packet	paquete (m)	4
paella	paella (valenciana) (f)	5
Pardon?	¿Perdón?	1
Paris	París	1
park	parque (m)	6
party	fiesta (f)	10
patio	patio (m)	9
patterned	estampado/a	4
pear	pera (f)	4
peas	guisantes (mpl)	4
people	gente (f)	10
pepper (condiment)	pimienta (f)	4
pepper (vegetable)	pimiento (m)	4
pessimistic	pesimista	3
phone, to	llamar por teléfono	9
piano	piano (m)	10
pink	rosa	4
plan, to	planear	9
plane	avión (m)	7
platform	andén (m)/vía (f)	7
play (an instrument), to	tocar	10
play, to	jugar	9
Pleased to meet you.	Encantado/a.	1
Pleased to meet you.	Mucho gusto.	3
pleasure	placer (m)	8
poor	pobre	3
pork	cerdo (m)	4
pork loin	cochinillo (m)	5
portion	ración (f)	5
Portuguese	portugués (-esa)	2
post office	correos (m)	6
postcode	código postal (m)	1

postwar	posguerra *(f)*	10	Rome	Roma	1	
prawns	gambas *(fpl)*	4	room	cuarto *(m)*	8	
precisely, on			room	habitación *(f)*	8	
the dot	en punto	7	run, to	correr	10	
prepare, to	preparar	9	Russia	Rusia *(f)*	2	
prepared	hecho/a	5	Russian	ruso/a	2	
present	regalo *(m)*	9				
pretty	guapo/a	3				
profession	profesión *(f)*	1				
province	provincia *(f)*	1	salad	ensalada *(f)*	5	
purple	púrpura	4	sale	liquidación *(f)*	4	
put, to	poner	10	sales	rebajas *(fpl)*	4	
			salmon	salmón *(m)*	4	
			salt	sal *(f)*	4	
quarter past	y cuarto	7	salted	salado/a	5	
quarter to	menos cuarto	7	sandals	sandalias *(fpl)*	4	
quick	rápido/a	7	Saturday	sábado *(m)*	7	
			say, to	decir	10	
			school	colegio *(m)*	2	
			scoop	bola *(f)*	5	
radio	radio *(f)*	10	scrambled eggs	revuelto *(m)*	5	
rain	lluvia *(f)*	6	scuba dive, to	bucear	10	
rain, to	llover	6	sea bream	besugo *(m)*	5	
raw	crudo/a	5	seafood	mariscos *(mpl)*	5	
reach, arrive			seasoned,			
(at) , to	llegar *(a)*	7	prepared	adobado/a	5	
reach, attain, to	alcanzar	10	second/main			
reception	recepción *(f)*	2	course	segundo plato *(m)*	5	
receptionist	recepcionista *(m/f)*	2	secretary	secretario/a *(m/f)*	2	
red	rojo/a	3	see, to	ver	9	
red wine	vino tinto *(m)*	4	seem, to	parecer	9	
red-haired	pelirrojo/a	3	sell, to	vender	4	
reservation	reserva *(f)*	9	sensitive	sensible	3	
reserved	reservada/o	5	September	septiembre *(m)*	7	
responsible	responsable	3	services	servicios *(mpl)*	8	
rest, to	descansar	9	several	varios/as	6	
restaurant	restaurante *(m)*	8	she	ella	1	
return	de ida y vuelta	7	shelves	estantería *(f)*	8	
rice	arroz *(m)*	4	shirt	camisa *(f)*	4	
rich	rico/a	3	shop	tienda *(f)*	6	
ride a bike, to	montar en bicicleta	10	shop window	escaparate *(m)*	4	
right; on the			short (height)	bajo/a	3	
right	derecha; a la derecha	6	short (length)	corto/a	3,4	
roast(ed)	asado/a	5	shower	ducha *(f)*	8	
roasted peppers	asadillo *(m)*	5	shy	tímido/a	3	
rolled in			sign, to	firmar	8	
(breadcrumbs)	rebozado/a	5	silk	seda *(f)*	4	

sincere	sincero/a	3
singer	cantante *(m/f)*	2
single	de ida	7
single (bed, etc.)	individual	8
single (not		
married)	soltero/a	3
sink (kitchen)	fregadero *(m)*	8
sir, Mr	señor *(m)*	1
sister	hermana *(f)*	3
size	talla *(f)*	4
skate, to	patinar	10
ski, go skiing, to	esquiar	9
skiing	esquí *(m)*	10
skirt	falda *(f)*	4
slim	delgado/a	3
small	pequeño/a	3,4
smoking	fumador	7
snow	nieve *(f)*	6
snow, to	nevar	6
sofa	sofá *(m)*	8
sole	lenguado *(m)*	5
some	algunos/as	6
sometimes	a veces	9
son	hijo *(m)*	3
sort, to	clasificar	9
so-so	regular	1
soup	sopa *(f)*	5
south	sur *(m)*	6
Spanish	español*(a)*	1
spicy sausage	chorizo *(m)*/	
	salchichón *(m)*	4
spinach	espinacas *(fpl)*	5
sport	deporte *(m)*	9
spotted	de lunares	4
spring	primavera *(f)*	6
square	plaza *(f)*	6
squid	calamares *(mpl)*	4
start, to	empezar	9
stationer's	papelería *(f)*	4
stay, to	quedar	9
story	historia *(f)*	10
straight	liso/a	3
straight on	todo recto	6
strawberry	fresa *(f)*	5
street	calle *(f)*	6
striped	de listas/de rayas	4

Q

R

S

strong	fuerte	3
student	estudiante *(m/f)*	1
study, to	estudiar	9
stuffed	relleno/a	5
stupid	tonto/a	3
subject	asunto *(m)*	8
sugar	azúcar *(m)*	4
summer	verano *(m)*	6
sunbathe, to	tomar el sol	9
Sunday	domingo *(m)*	7
surgery	clínica *(f)*	2
surname	apellido *(m)*	1,3
surrounding area	alrededores *(mpl)*	6
sweater	jersey *(m)*	4
swim, to	nadar	9
swimming pool	piscina *(f)*	6,10
swordfish	pez espada *(m)*	5

T

take a nap, to	echarse la siesta	9
take, eat, drink, to	tomar	5,6
take, to	coger	6
talk, speak, to	hablar	2
tall	alto/a	3
taxi	taxi *(m)*	10
taxi driver	taxista *(m/f)*	2
tea	té *(m)*	4
teacher	profesor(a) *(m/f)*	1,2
team	equipo *(m)*	10
telephone (number)	teléfono *(m)*	1
tennis	tenis *(m)*	9
terrace	terraza *(f)*	9
terrible	fatal	1
Thank you.	Gracias.	1
that/those	ese/esa/esos/esas	4
that/those	ése/ésa/ésos/ésas	4
that/those (over there)	aquel/aquella/ aquellos/aquellas	4
the day after tomorrow	pasado mañana	9
the day before yesterday	anteayer	10
the Philippines	Filipinas *(fpl)*	2
the United States	Estados Unidos *(mpl)*	4
The weather's bad.	Hace mal tiempo.	6

The weather's nice.	Hace buen tiempo.	6
theatre	teatro *(m)*	6
then	luego/seguidamente	9
third	tercero/a	6
this/these	este/esta/estos/estas	4
this/these	éste/ésta/éstos/éstas	3,4
Thursday	jueves *(m)*	7
ticket	billete *(m)* (Sp)/ boleto *(m)* (LA)	7
tight	estrecho/a	4
tin	lata *(f)*	4
tip	propina *(f)*	5
to	a	7
tobacconist's	estanco *(m)*	4
today	hoy	7
together	junto/a	10
toilet	wáter *(m)*	8
toilet paper	papel higiénico *(m)*	8
toilets	servicios *(mpl)*	8
tomato	tomate *(m)*	4
tomorrow	mañana	7
too (much/ many)	demasiado/a	10
tourist information office	oficina de información *(f)*	6
towel	toalla *(f)*	8
town	pueblo *(m)*	6
town hall	ayuntamiento *(m)*	6
train	tren *(m)*	7
train station	estación de tren *(f)*	6
transfer	traslado *(m)*	9
trousers	pantalones *(mpl)*	4
try, to	probar	4
Tuesday	martes *(m)*	7
tuna	atún *(m)*	4
turn, to	doblar/torcer	6
TV	televisión *(f)*	8
typical	típico/a	5

U

ugly	feo/a	3
unbelievable	increíble	9
uncle	tío *(m)*	3
under	debajo de	6
underground station	metro *(m)*	6

university	universidad *(f)*	9
unkind	antipático/a	3
until	hasta	7
usually	por lo general	9

V

varied	variado/a	5
various	varios/as	6
veal	ternera *(f)*	4
vegetables	verduras *(fpl)*	4
vermouth	vermut *(m)*	5
very well	muy bien	1
via, by way of	vía	7
village	pueblo *(m)*	6
vinegar	vinagre *(m)*	5
visit	visita *(f)*	9
visit, to	visitar	7

W

waiter/waitress	camarero/a *(m/f)*	2
walk, stroll, to	pasear	10
walk, to	andar	6
walking, on foot	andando	6
want, to	querer	4
wanted (to buy)	se compra	9
wash (oneself), to	lavarse	9
washbasin	lavabo *(m)*	8
washing machine	lavadora *(f)*	8
weak	débil	3
wear, to	llevar	4,5
Wednesday	miércoles *(m)*	7
week	semana *(f)*	7
weekend	fin de semana *(m)*	9
welcome	bienvenido/a	9
well	bien	1
well known	conocido/a	10
west	oeste *(m)*	6
what	qué	2
What a shame!	¡Qué pena!	4
What do you do?	¿Qué hace(s)?	2
What is …?	¿Cuál es …?	1
What would you like?	¿Qué desea?	4
What's your name? (formal)	¿Cómo se llama?	1
where	dónde	2
Where are you from?	¿De dónde eres/es?	1,2

white	blanco/a	4
white wine	vino blanco *(m)*	4
widowed	viudo/a	3
wife	mujer *(f)*	3
wild mushrooms	setas *(fpl)*	5
win, to	ganar	10
wine glass	copa *(f)*	5
wish, want, to	desear	4
with a sea view	con vista al mar	9
with grated cheese	gratinado/a	5
with me	conmigo	2
with you	contigo	2
woman	mujer *(f)*	3
wool	lana *(f)*	4
work, to	trabajar	2

Y

year	año *(m)*	2,8
yellow	amarillo/a	4
yes	sí	1
yesterday	ayer	10
yoghurt	yogur *(m)*	4
you (formal)	usted	1
you (informal)	tú	1
your	vuestro/a	8
your (formal)	su	3
your (formal)	su	1
your (informal)	tu	1,3
youth hostel	albergue juvenil *(m)*	8